kid chef bakes

kid chef BAKES

The KIDS COOKBOOK FOR ASPIRING BAKERS

Lisa Huff

ROCKRIDGE PRESS

For general information on our other products and services or to obtain technical support, please contact our Customer Care Department within the U.S. at (866) 744-2665, or outside the U.S. at (510) 253-0500.

Rockridge Press publishes its books in a variety of electronic and print formats. Some content that appears in print may not be available in electronic books, and vice versa.

TRADEMARKS: Rockridge Press and the Rockridge Press logo are trademarks or registered trademarks of Callisto Media Inc. and/or its affiliates, in the United States and other countries, and may not be used without written permission. All other trademarks are the property of their respective owners. Rockridge Press is not associated with any product or vendor mentioned in this book.

All photography © Hélène Dujardin/Food styling by Tami Hardeman/prop styling by Angela Hall except pages 34, 72 & 83: © Jennifer Davick; pages 67, 77, 79, 93, 117, 125, 135, 145, 151, 163, 173, 177 & 187: © Lisa Huff; page 133: Ellie Baygulov/Stocksy. Illustrations: TongSur/iStock, pages 11-13.
Author photo © Andrea Topalian

ISBN: Print 978-1-62315-942-9 | eBook 978-1-62315-943-6

To my kids, Jordan and Cora,
and all other kids learning to bake.
Keep baking, and may all your
dreams come true!

CONTENTS

INTRODUCTION

Welcome to the world of baking! Okay, you may have been baking in the kitchen for years with your grandparents, parents, older siblings, or maybe even all by yourself. So now you have this book—with all these tools, you're off to a great start! If you're just getting started baking in the kitchen, that's awesome, too! This fun book will teach you baking basics, and also help you master some more advanced baking techniques.

When we think of baking, most of us conjure up images of cookies, breads, cakes, pies—well, desserts! That's definitely part of it, but other baking options that we'll explore include appetizers, pizzas, and quiche, to name a few. At its core, baking is the act of cooking something, usually flour-based foods, with dry heat (like in an oven). Baking is a little different than cooking, and sometimes trickier! With many baking recipes, there is a science behind the recipe. Finding the right balance between ingredients can be a challenge. Like, when I was a kid, I thought I could substitute melted butter for softened butter in one of my favorite cookie recipes. What a disaster—my cookies turned out flat and mushy and fell apart! I quickly learned that shortcuts aren't always a great idea when baking. I'll share some of my funny and memorable lessons with you so you can hopefully learn from my mistakes, which, by the way, weren't so funny at the time.

This book will help you learn lessons for baking success, as well as many baking tricks and tips along the way that might surprise your older family members, as well! Get ready to:

- Explore your kitchen and learn what baking tools, appliances, bakeware, cookware, and pantry items can really help make you a baking pro.

- Master baking skills such as how to measure ingredients, mix and fold, cream butter and sugar, create perfect dough, and melt chocolate, so you'll be ready to move onto more advanced baking recipes in no time.

- Discover a world of sweet and savory baking recipes you can try, from basic to more advanced delicacies, as well as classics to new favorites.

Let's get baking—you'll soon see it's "a piece of cake!"

PART ONE

welcome to baking school!

1

in the baker's kitchen

Your mouth may be watering with the idea of yummy baked goods, but first, let's make sure you have everything you need in your kitchen to get started, including basic baking equipment, ingredients, and some general rules and tips to get you prepared and keep you safe. I'm also sharing some of my favorite baking gear and tool ideas, and I hope you'll discover some of your own favorites, as you begin to explore the joys of baking.

KITCHEN RULES

Rules aren't fun, but these few simple rules will keep you safe and avoid another irksome fate—unnecessary cleanup! Here's a quick list of things to keep in mind before you start baking.

1. **Check in with an adult**. Before you start baking, check in with an adult. It's a good idea for someone to know what you're doing and where you are, especially in case of an emergency.

2. **Wash hands**. Every good chef makes a habit of washing their hands with warm soapy water before getting started in the kitchen, and then again before and after handling raw meat (and of course when their hands get messy while baking). I realize that it's tough to resist licking frosting off your fingers; just make sure you're done handling the food before you reward yourself with that treat!

3. **Prepare a chef-worthy work area.** Find a counter or table that has plenty of room to work at and to hold your ingredients and tools. Give the area a quick cleaning with a warm soapy sponge and dry with a clean towel.

   > **KID CHEF TIP:** Keep baking soda nearby, as it can also serve as a fire extinguisher. Pouring baking soda on a small oven fire can smother the blaze.

4. **Wash ingredients.** Washing and drying any fresh fruit or vegetables will get rid of some of the dirt, germs, and chemicals used in farming. Some produce might require scrubbing the dirt off with a soft brush.

5. **Prep like a pro.** Give your recipe a quick read through and make sure you understand all the steps in the recipe. Ensure that you have everything you need by gathering your ingredients, bakeware, and tools. This is known as *mise en place* (pronounced MEEZ ahn plahs), French for "everything in its place."

6. **Clean as you go.** I hate cleaning, too, but if you keep your work area clean as you go, it will mean less cleanup when you're done baking.

7. **Be prepared for an emergency.** Talk with an adult about what to do in case of a fire or an emergency in the kitchen. It's good to know where the fire extinguisher is located and how to use it, just in case it's needed.

BAKER'S PANTRY

Your pantry is where the ingredients await! And the first rule of thumb for delicious baked goods: start with quality ingredients. It's important to have the right ingredients, but it's just as important that your ingredients are fresh and of the best quality. In some cases, you can substitute ingredients when you don't have the right thing, but sometimes substituting ingredients in baked goods can have disappointing results. Here are some common ingredients used in many baking recipes.

Baking Powder

This powder is a leavening agent—it makes baked goods rise. Store this in a dry, dark, cool place. You can check the expiration date, but it should usually be replaced every six to twelve months. Here's a fun experiment to test if baking powder is still good: Stir about 1 teaspoon baking powder into 1/3 cup hot water. If the mixture produces a lot of bubbles, the baking powder is still good to use.

Baking Soda

Similar to baking powder, baking soda is a leavening agent used to make baked goods rise. Baking soda and baking powder are not the same and can't be substituted for one another. Unlike baking powder, baking soda needs an acid in the recipe to make it work. You can check the expiration date, but baking soda also needs to be replaced every six to twelve months. A fun way to test if baking soda is still good: Stir about 1 teaspoon of baking soda into 1/3 cup of something acidic, such as lemon juice or vinegar. If the mixture produces lots of bubbles, the baking soda is still good to use.

Butter

Butter is used in many baking recipes. There are two main types of butter, unsalted and salted. Most baking recipes will call for unsalted butter, so you can control the amount of salt by adding it separately. Check your recipe to see if the butter should be cold, softened to room temperature, or melted. Don't substitute one for another, even if you're in a hurry. Also, don't substitute margarine or oil for butter unless the recipe says it's okay. Butter can be kept at room temperature for a short amount of time, but generally should be kept refrigerated.

Chocolate

This wildly popular delicacy comes in many types: unsweetened, dark, bittersweet, and semisweet are some of the most common. Unsweetened chocolate (which doesn't taste so great by itself) usually comes in bar form, while dark, bittersweet, and semisweet can be found as chips or bars. Unsweetened cocoa powder is called for in some baking recipes. This is a powder and contains no sugar. Chocolate lasts for a long time, but for best results, it should be stored in a dry, dark, cool place. Storing chocolate in the fridge is not recommended because the chocolate may "bloom," forming a gray film on the outside caused by the cocoa butter separating from the chocolate. It's safe to eat, but not so pretty to look at!

Cream and Milk

Whipped cream, made from cream, is a yummy and festive addition over many baked goods. If you're not familiar with cream, look out for the different types of cream next time you're in the grocery store. Heavy cream is the richest type of liquid cream, made up of at least 36 percent fat. Whipping cream has a fat content between 30 and 36 percent. Heavy cream and whipping cream should both be stored in the refrigerator. Either can be used in most cases, but whipping heavy cream will result in a more stable, slightly thicker whipped cream.

Milk also comes in different fat contents. Whole milk is the highest in fat, followed by 2 percent, 1 percent, and then skim (fat-free). When baking with milk, a higher fat content milk will result in a moister and finer-textured baked good.

With both cream and milk, check the expiration date on the container before using; a sniff test will also tell you if your dairy is past its freshness. In general, both cream and milk should be used within two weeks of opening.

SEASONAL FOOD CHOICES

There's a good reason apple pie is associated with fall: apples are simply at their best, so crispy and juicy! This formula holds true for all kinds of baked goods—everything has its season. Whenever possible, use fresh fruits and vegetables in your baked goods. You can sometimes substitute frozen or canned, but for best results, there's nothing like fresh produce, and especially when it's in season. When choosing fresh produce, look for fruits and vegetables that are ripe and free of wrinkles and blemishes. Most produce can be found in grocery stores year-round, but here's a quick list of some popular baking produce and their peak seasons throughout the year.

FALL
- Apples
- Bananas
- Cranberries
- Pears
- Pineapple
- Pumpkins
- Sweet Potatoes

WINTER
- Bananas
- Lemons
- Pears
- Sweet potatoes

SPRING
- Apricots
- Bananas
- Mangos
- Pineapple
- Rhubarb
- Strawberries

SUMMER
- Apricots
- Bananas
- Blackberries
- Blueberries
- Cherries
- Peaches
- Plums
- Raspberries
- Strawberries
- Zucchini

Eggs

Eggs add so much to baked goods, including richness, color, strength, and structure. Eggs come in different sizes (medium, large, X-large, jumbo, etc.) and colors (brown and white). The standard egg size for most baking recipes is large unless otherwise directed. Egg color does not matter—white and brown eggs can be used interchangeably. Eggs may also be pasteurized or unpasteurized. Unpasteurized eggs may contain bacteria, so they should never be consumed raw. Use pasteurized eggs for any recipe in which the eggs are not fully cooked. Store eggs in the refrigerator and check the expiration date on the egg carton before using.

Flour

Flour is not just flour anymore! Many types of flour are sold today including all-purpose (bleached or unbleached), bread, cake, and whole-wheat, as well as specialty flours such as almond, coconut, etc., which are not made of grains. The type of flour to use is usually stated in the recipe (this cookbook mostly calls for all-purpose flour), and other types shouldn't be used interchangeably unless the recipe specifies it's okay.

Sifting flour (running the flour through a sieve or sifter) will break up any lumps and it also aerates (adds air to) the flour. This extra step is mostly unnecessary for everyday baking, but it can be helpful for delicate baked goods such as angel food and sponge cakes.

Flour should be stored in an airtight container in a dark, dry, cool place. Whole-grain flours, if not being used for a while, can be stored in the freezer to prolong shelf life and keep the oils from going bad.

KID CHEF TIP: Check an egg's freshness with a float test. Place the egg in a container of cold water. If the egg lies at the bottom on its side, it's really fresh. If it stands in the bottom, it's still fresh enough to use. If it floats to the top, it's no longer fresh enough to eat.

Spices

Spices are fun because they add unique flavors and aromas to baked goods. These can remind us of holidays as they fill our homes with their delightful scents! Some of the most common spices used for baking include cinnamon, cloves, ginger, nutmeg, allspice, and even salt. There are also spice blends that are worth discovering and great for baking, such as apple pie and pumpkin pie spice. Many spices can be used interchangeably, but your baked treat will have a different taste depending on what you use. Ground dried spices may start to lose some of their flavor after about six months, but are still safe to use. Spices should be stored away from heat in a dry, dark, cool place.

Sugar

Like flour, sugar comes in many types, such as granulated, confectioners' (powdered), light and dark brown, and even some more exotic varieties like turbinado and muscovado. Granulated, powdered, and brown sugar are the most well-known and commonly used in everyday baking. Light and dark brown sugar can be used interchangeably, but dark brown sugar will give your baked goods a stronger molasses flavor. Sugar should be stored in airtight containers in a dry, dark, cool place.

Vanilla

Vanilla extract is great for everyday baking since it's a quick and easy way to add deeper flavor. Vanilla extract is made by infusing vanilla beans into alcohol—this is why vanilla extract smells great but tastes pretty terrible by itself! Vanilla beans can also be used. They are more expensive, but are great to use in recipes if you want a stronger vanilla flavor. Both vanilla extract and vanilla beans should be stored in a dry, dark, cool place.

BAKING EQUIPMENT

I'm going to share some of my favorite cookware, bakeware, tools, utensils, and small appliances with you. I've accumulated them over the years, but these are all good basics to start with on your way to becoming a baking pro. There is also a world of cool specialty bakeware items and equipment that are fun and unique, but the following items will help you get started.

COOKWARE AND BAKEWARE

 Baking dishes Deep square, oblong, or rectangular baking pans used for cakes, cobblers, and other baked goods. Usually made of metal, glass, or ceramic.

 Baking sheets Large, flat rectangular metal pans (preferably rimmed to avoid dripping) for baking cookies, pastries, biscuits, and other baked goods. Baking sheets come in full, three-quarter, half, and quarter sizes. I prefer the half size (13-by-18-inch) for most baking jobs, and it fits most conventional ovens.

 Cake pans Round metal pans normally used to bake cakes. They may also be used to bake other things that cook snugly together, such as cinnamon rolls.

 Double boiler Two saucepans fitted together with boiling water in the bottom pan. Typically used for melting chocolate, as well as making custards and some sauces. (See Make Your Own Double Boiler, page 53.)

 Loaf pans Deep, narrow, rectangular pans generally used to bake—you guessed it—breads and loaf cakes. Loaf pans can be made out of metal, glass, or ceramic, and your results may vary depending on the type of loaf pan you use.

 Muffin pans Baking pans with built-in cups, primarily for making muffins and cupcakes, but sometimes even cookies. Usually made out of metal or silicone, these come in different sizes, including mini, standard, and jumbo.

 Pie pans Round baking pans made out of metal, glass, or ceramic. Generally used to make pies and quiches, but may also be used for other baked goods.

 Ramekins Small dishes made out of ceramic or sometimes glass. Used for making individual portions.

Skillet A shallow metal pan with many uses, including cooking food on the stovetop or baking in the oven. Cast-iron skillets are my personal favorite because they retain heat well and can be used both on the stovetop and in the oven. They are, however, pretty heavy.

 Tube pan A deep, metal, circular-shaped baking pan with a hole in the middle. Mostly used to bake cakes such as angel food and coffee cakes.

TOOLS & UTENSILS

 Cookie cutters You can find cookie cutters in almost every theme, from holidays to animals. Besides all the fun shapes and sizes out there, round and square cookie cutters in various sizes come in handy for cutting out cookies, pastries, and even biscuits.

 Grater A tool with many small blades on its surface. Used for shredding cheese, vegetables, and other foods.

 Measuring cups Cups of various sizes used to measure liquid or dry ingredients.

 Measuring spoons Spoons of various sizes used to measure small amounts of liquid or dry ingredients.

 Mixing bowls Bowls of different sizes, used to mix and combine ingredients together.

 Pastry brush A small, flat brush used for jobs like brushing butter or eggs onto baked goods, or brushing crumbs off cakes before frosting.

 Pastry cutter A tool, generally made of narrow metal strips attached to a handle, used to mix or "cut" butter or shortening into flour to make biscuits, pie crusts, and pastry dough. (See Cutting in Butter, page 42.)

 Peeler A small kitchen tool with a sharp blade that peels skin off vegetables or fruit.

 Rolling pin A long cylinder-shaped kitchen tool with handles, used for rolling out dough for cookies, pies, and pizza.

 Spatula A flat, handled kitchen utensil that comes in a variety of shapes and sizes. Used for spreading and mixing, or lifting baked goods. Heat-resistant spatulas are best for baking.

Spring-loaded scoops A utensil with a trigger release that is perfect for scooping equal-sized measurements of batter and dough for such things as cookies, cupcakes, and muffins. It's nice to have a small and large one.

 Whisk A kitchen utensil with wire loops held together by a handle, used for beating, whipping, or mixing ingredients.

 Wooden spoon A strong spoon perfect for scraping and mixing in ingredients that can't be beaten in with an electric mixer.

 Zester A sharp kitchen utensil used to take the zest off citrus fruit or grate whole spices.

APPLIANCES

 Blender An electric appliance with a tall glass or plastic container that has sharp blades at the bottom, used to purée, chop, or mix foods. A great tool to make quick fruit sauces for baked goods.

 Food processor An electric appliance with a holding canister and interchangeable blades, used for slicing, shredding, and chopping. Useful for quickly mixing dough and chopping nuts, cookies, and crackers into crumbs.

 Hand mixer A small handheld electric appliance with a set of rotating beaters. Used to beat, whip, and mix ingredients. Great for more control and speed in beating your ingredients.

 Stand mixer An electric appliance with a mixer over a bowl on a platform that comes with a variety of attachments, such as beaters, dough hooks, spatulas, and whisks for hands-free mixing. Great choice for recipes that require long mixing times.

KNIVES AND OTHER SHARP TOOLS

To make your work easier, you'll need a few good knives and sharp tools in your kitchen. It's helpful to know the best uses for different types of knives, as well as other sharp tools such as graters and peelers. Good kitchen tools can make things quicker and easier in the kitchen, but discuss their use with an adult beforehand, and then use caution when handling.

KID CHEF TIP: Place a damp cloth or towel under your cutting board to prevent it from sliding while cutting.

Know Your Knives

There are four types of knife that will help you with your baking. Each one has a special use, and you will find that using the right knife can make your job easier.

- **Butter knife** A small knife with a blunt-edge blade. Great to use for slicing soft food or spreading foods such as peanut butter, butter, cream cheese, etc.

- **Chef's knife** An all-purpose knife with a large, sharp, straight-edge blade. Used for a wide variety of purposes such as chopping, dicing, and slicing food.

- **Paring knife** A small knife with a sharp, straight blade. Generally used for peeling and coring food. Also good for finely cutting small amounts of food such as fresh fruits, vegetables, and herbs.

- **Serrated knife** A knife with a sharp saw-like edge. Typically used to slice through bread. Smaller versions can also be used to slice through such food as tomatoes and pineapple.

CUTTING STYLES

A **Chop.** To cut food into small, similar-sized pieces. Chopped food should be uniform in size and may be finely chopped (small pieces) or coarsely chopped (larger pieces), depending on the recipe.

B **Dice.** To cut food into small cubes. Size may vary but generally from about ¼-inch to ¾-inch in diameter.

C **Julienne.** To cut food into long thin uniform sized strips, like matchsticks.

D **Mince.** To cut food into very small similar sized pieces and smaller than chopped food.

E **Slice.** To cut food into thin pieces that are similar thickness.

How to Use a Knife

Learning how to hold and use a knife can take some practice. If you're just starting out, ask an adult to help you get started and demonstrate how to hold and use a knife properly.

- **Choose the right knife for the job.** Different knives have different jobs (see Know Your Knives, page 14), so be sure you have the correct size and shape when starting.

- **Use two hands.** Are you a righty or a lefty? Your dominant hand should hold the knife, while your less dominant hand carefully holds the food in place.

- **Hold the knife based on its size.** For larger knives, wrap your fingers around the handle, curling your pointer finger up against the blade for better control. For smaller knives, wrap your fingers around the handle, and if it helps, place your pointer finger on top of the knife for better control.

KNIFE SAFETY

- **Sharpen knives.** Does your home have a knife sharpener? Sharpening knives ensures easy food preparation and can even prevent accidents such as knives slipping while cutting.

- **Use a cutting board.** Don't hold food in your hands while you try to cut it. A cutting board will help prevent the knife from slipping while cutting, and of course, you want the knife to connect with the board—not with your skin!

- **Watch your fingers.** Keep your fingers tucked in and focus on what you're doing to prevent injuries.

- **Carry and store knives correctly.** Carry knives by the handle with the tip down and blade facing away from you and others. Knives should be stored in a knife rack or knife drawer.

- **Keep your knives clean.** Make sure your knives are clean and handles are dry and free from anything greasy. Take care not to leave knives in the sink or where someone could grab them accidentally.

- **Read what size to cut.** Check the recipe to see what needs to be chopped, minced, or sliced (see Cutting Styles, page 15).

- **Watch your fingers!** When you're slicing, tuck in your fingers and place your knuckles against the knife to steer it. Keep your hands and fingers stable to make even slices, and call on a grown-up to help if you need assistance—hard foods like carrots can be tough to cut through.

USING THE STOVE

Every stove is a little different. If you are unsure how to use your specific stove, ask an adult or parent for help—they will probably be able to tell you more about your stove. Gas (which have a stovetop flame) and electric stoves (which have a coil or surface that turns red hot) are also a little different from each other in the way they cook.

Always make sure your stovetop is clean before you turn it on. A dirty stovetop with grease or leftover food can start a fire. It's also best to place your pot or pan on the burner before lighting or turning it on.

Heat for the stovetop is usually controlled by a knob or digital panel on your stove for each specific burner. Heat can range between low (or 1) and high (or 10). Gas stoves have pilot lights, which are flames that burn continuously under the surface of the stovetop. To light the burner, turn the knob to "light" until you hear a clicking sound and see a flame. Now you can adjust the heat. If the gas burner doesn't light right away, turn it off for a few moments so you don't let gas escape—this can cause a fire and release harmful carbon monoxide.

Whether you have a gas or electric stove, there are some safety tips that even the most seasoned chefs follow:

- Make sure handles from pots and pans are always facing in, and not over the edge of the stove, where someone can accidentally knock them over or smaller children can grab them.

- Know where the fire extinguisher is kept. If you put water on a grease fire, it can get bigger and spread, so when in doubt, use a fire extinguisher or even baking soda if needed.

- Use sturdy oven mitts or potholders to prevent burns when handling or working with hot pans and pots. Also use mitts or potholders when stirring with metal spoons or utensils—they can quickly heat up when in contact with something hot.

- Pull your hair back, and make sure you are not wearing any loose clothing, long sleeves, or jewelry that may catch fire or get caught.

- Don't get distracted! Even the best chefs have learned from experience—never leave a pan unattended on the stove. Keep an eye on whatever you are cooking.

USING THE OVEN

Just like stovetops, every oven can be a little different depending on age, model, and type. There are two major types: conventional and convection. A conventional oven is designed with two heating elements: one for baking and one for broiling. A convection oven uses circulating hot, dry air to create a more even heat and faster baking times, and is generally used for baked items. The times and temperatures in these recipes are designed for conventional ovens, so if you're using a convection oven, you may need to adjust your baking temperature and/or time for many of the recipes.

Before you use the oven, do a quick inspection to make sure the inside of your oven is clean and nothing has been left inside such as pans, food, or anything that could catch fire or burn. After your inspection, adjust the oven racks to wherever you would like them. Typically, placing your rack in the middle of the oven, and placing the pan in the middle of that rack results in the most even heat. However, if you need to put more than one pan in the oven and need more than one rack, you can place two oven racks equally apart and, if you wish, rotate pans halfway through baking for more even cooking and browning.

When you're ready to turn on the oven, look at the panel on top of the stove. Many ovens now have a digital panel. Either way, enter or turn

TIMER TO THE RESCUE!

I still sometimes get distracted in the kitchen and forget that I have something in the oven. I have burned many things—nuts, brownies, bread, you name it! Now I try to always set a timer even if I think I'll remember. It's a true recipe saver!

the dial to the desired temperature, and fully preheat your oven before placing your baked goods inside. After you place your baked goods in the oven, use a timer to remind you to check on your food—it's easy to forget something's baking!

Every oven is different. Baking and cooking times listed in a recipe are reasonable suggestions, but can vary by a few minutes or more. For best results, keep an eye on what you're baking and check on it every few minutes.

Don't worry if you need to bake things a little less or a little longer on occasion than what is suggested in the recipe. However, if you feel that your oven always seems to be baking things much quicker or slower than it should, an inexpensive oven thermometer will allow you to double-check that your oven is heating correctly.

Just like when using the stovetop, a few basic safety guidelines can prevent oven fires and accidents:

- Know where a fire extinguisher is stored (or baking soda).

- Stand back when opening the door to a hot oven. The steamy air coming out of the oven can be quite hot.

- Make sure no small children are nearby when opening the oven.

- Use oven mitts or potholders whenever placing pans in the oven or taking them out.

- Keep pans and food away from the heating elements in the oven. If things are too close to the heating elements, they can catch fire.

- Make sure anything you put in the oven, such as pots, pans, paper liners, etc., are oven-safe for use at high temperatures.

- Be careful when dealing with hot objects in the kitchen. Good oven mitts are essential so you don't burn yourself, but also use caution when placing hot objects on other surfaces like countertops, tables, or surfaces that may crack, stain, etc.

MY BAKER'S DOZEN TIPS

A baker's dozen is 13. If you're in a bakery that offers a baker's dozen, that means you'll get one free when you order 12 of something. That said, here are 13 of my overall top tips to help you become a baking pro!

1 **Buy the freshest and best quality ingredients you can.** The better the ingredients, the better your results will be. It makes sense—if you're starting with ingredients that don't taste good, your baked goods won't taste good either!

2 **Start with easy recipes.** Begin with ones that you are comfortable with, and then step up to recipes that are a little bit more challenging each time you bake.

3 **Read through the recipe before starting.** Make sure you understand every step and have all the ingredients, bakeware, and tools needed to complete the recipe.

4 **Ask questions.** If you don't understand the recipe or how to do something directed in the recipe, ask an adult for help.

5 **Find a work area that has plenty of room.** Clean your hands and your work area before starting, and keep the area clean as you go.

6 **Put safety first.** Practice good safety skills and keep an eye on what you're doing to prevent accidents and fires.

7 **Get organized.** Remember *mise en place*, "everything in its place?" It's a great skill to practice—pretend you're on a cooking show! Get all your ingredients, bakeware, and tools in order before starting. Prep all your ingredients so you're ready to go.

10 **Be watchful.** Cooking times can vary so keep an eye on things. Look for visual clues like browning or bubbling, or try inserting a toothpick into the middle of some baked goods, like brownies or cakes, to see if they're done.

11 **Use a timer.** Let it help remind you when to check on what you're baking.

12 **Don't get frustrated.** If things don't turn out quite as you planned, take a deep breath. It's okay, mishaps will occur—remember my mushy cookie story? Learn from what went wrong, and try again.

13 **Have fun!** Baking should be an enjoyable adventure!

8 **Be cautious when substituting ingredients.** Baking is a science. Not all ingredients can be substituted for others with similar results. Sometimes an Internet search will offer suggestions for a reasonable substitution, but the results will vary depending on what you're making.

9 **Measure with care.** Take your time and look at your measuring cup with a level eye. An inaccurate measurement can mean the difference between yum and yuck!

2

baking skills

Now that you have done inventory of your basic cookware, bakeware, utensils, and tools, let's discuss how you can use some of them. There is definitely some science and chemistry involved with baked goods— remember those fun experiments to see if your baking soda and powder are still good? You'll be prepared to make perfectly baked goods after we explore some basic techniques, such as how to measure ingredients, cream butter and sugar, melt chocolate, and more!

THE BASICS

Before we get to mixing and baking, it's good to know a few basics. One of the most important things to know is how to measure liquid and dry ingredients. It's also good to know other tricks, such as preparing different temperatures of butter, greasing a pan, and knowing when your baked goods are done.

Measuring Liquids

Transparent measuring cups are best to use for larger amounts of liquids; measuring spoons work for smaller amounts. Pour liquids directly into the measuring cup and place on a flat surface such as your counter. Here's the trick: To check your measurement, be sure to bend down and look at the liquid at eye level. Looking from below or above can result in a miscalculation. When using measuring spoons, fill the spoon until it's level and flat all the way across.

 KID CHEF TIP:
For sticky liquids such as honey or molasses, spray your measuring cup or spoon with a little nonstick spray before measuring to keep the liquid from sticking. It should pour right out into your mixing bowl.

Measuring Dry Ingredients

The most accurate method for measuring dry ingredients is by using a scale and measuring by weight, not volume, especially for flour. However, most recipes call for measuring by volume (including those in this book). Use dry measuring cups for larger amounts of dry ingredients, and measuring spoons for smaller amounts. Dry measuring cups are typically opaque (not transparent) and made of metal or plastic.

To measure flour, lightly spoon the flour directly into the measuring cup. Using the flat side of a butter knife, gently scrape the excess off so the flour is level with the measuring cup.

Brown sugar is usually measured by packing the brown sugar into the measuring cup tightly, unless otherwise noted. You can press it down so it's level, or with the flat side of a butter knife, gently scrape off the excess to make it level.

For most other dry ingredients, you can use the measuring cup to scoop up the ingredients and shake it a bit until level with the measuring cup.

Melting or Softening Butter

When using butter, check to see if the recipe calls for cold, melted, or room-temperature softened butter. They should not be used interchangeably.

- **Melted.** Butter can be melted in a small saucepan on the stove, or in the microwave in a microwave-safe container lightly covered to prevent spattering—you won't want to clean *that* up!

- **Softened.** For room-temperature butter, let the butter sit on the counter for at least a half hour, or until it's soft to the touch. Some microwaves even have a "soften" setting.

- **Cold.** Leave the butter in the fridge until ready to use. Most times, you'll need to cut the butter into small cubes if using it cold.

Greasing a Pan

Recipes generally call for either a greased or ungreased pan. Depending on your pan, how you grease it may vary. Nonstick and silicone bakeware do not usually need to be greased. For other pans, there are several options. You can lightly spray the pan with a nonstick spray. You can lightly spread some room-temperature butter or shortening on the pan with a paper towel. Or you can line the pan with parchment paper or nonstick foil. Greasing or lining a pan keeps cookies and biscuits from sticking to the pan and makes baked goods such as cakes, bars, and brownies easier to remove.

Some recipes, such as cakes and brownies, may direct you to butter *and* flour the pan. First, grease the pan with butter or shortening on a paper towel. Then lightly spoon some flour over the pan and gently shake it around until it's well coated. Turn the pan upside down over a sink and lightly tap the pan on the sink to remove excess flour.

KID CHEF TIP:
DO: If you're making a chocolate baked good, you can add a little cocoa powder to the flour, before flouring the pan. **DON'T:** When making Angel Food Cake (page 90), don't grease the pan. The cake needs to stick to the sides in order to rise!

very berry granola bars

PREP TIME: 20 minutes

COOK TIME: 34 minutes

YIELD: 8 bars

TOOLS/EQUIPMENT

- 8-inch square baking pan
- Parchment paper or aluminum foil
- Large saucepan

⅓ cup unsalted butter

⅓ cup honey

2 tablespoons brown sugar

1 teaspoon vanilla extract

¼ teaspoon table salt

2 cups quick rolled oats

½ cup chopped almonds (see Pro Tip)

¾ cup chopped dried chewy fruit

Preheat the oven to 350°F.

Line an 8-by-8-inch square baking pan, including sides, with parchment paper or aluminum foil.

Melt the butter and sugar.

In a large saucepan over medium heat, heat the butter, honey, brown sugar, vanilla, and salt. Cook 3 to 4 minutes, stirring occasionally, until blended and smooth.

Add the oats.

Remove the pan from the heat. Add the oats, almonds, and dried fruit to the pan, stirring to combine.

Bake the bars.

Spoon the mixture into the prepared pan. With the back of a fork, firmly press down on the mixture to form an even layer in the pan. Bake for 25 to 30 minutes, or until brown and toasted.

Cool and cut the bars.

Remove the pan from the oven. Press firmly again on the mixture with the back of a fork. Cool completely overnight, covered. Remove from pan and cut into bars.

PRO TIP: To easily chop almonds, place them in a resealable bag, then smack them with a rolling pin or the flat side of a meat tenderizer until they reach the desired consistency.

CRACKING AND SEPARATING EGGS

If you've never cracked an egg, it's a great skill to practice since so many recipes require eggs. There are several methods that can be used to crack eggs—even one-handed, if you practice! Some recipes may also call for egg whites and/or egg yolks, so learning how to separate eggs is also an egg-ceptional skill for any young chef.

Room-Temperature Eggs

It's usually best to crack and separate eggs straight out of the fridge, while the eggs are still cold. After you crack or separate your eggs into a bowl, let them sit on the counter for about a half hour to reach room temperature. Room-temperature eggs and egg whites will become a little fluffier when whipped, so if you have the time, test whipping room-temperature eggs versus cold ones and see if you notice a difference.

Cracking Eggs

There are several popular ways to crack an egg. One way is to crack it on the side of a bowl. Separate the shell at the crack and pour the egg into a bowl. Another method is to tap the egg gently on a flat, hard surface to crack the egg and then pour the egg into a bowl.

It's also a good idea to crack your eggs over a separate bowl, rather than over a mixing bowl containing other ingredients. It's easier to get the shell out of a little bowl with nothing else in it than from a mixing bowl with other ingredients. To remove the shell, you can use a small spoon or fork, or wet your finger with a little water and pull the shell pieces out. With a little patience, it should all come out. If you use your finger to get the shell out, be sure to wash your hands again so you don't get bacteria on your hands.

> **KID CHEF TIP:**
> Tapping an egg on a flat hard surface (rather than on a side of a bowl) will usually get less egg shell in your bowl!

Separating Eggs

Some recipes may require just egg whites or egg yolks, rather than the whole egg. You can use specialty tools to separate eggs, but it's a fun trick to just use the egg shell. Here's how: Start with cold eggs because they are easier to separate. Crack the egg in the middle of the shell, then gently open the egg over a bowl, letting the yolk rest in one side of the shell while the whites drip over the edge of the shell into the bowl. Gently transfer the yolk back and forth between the two shells until the white is completely in the bowl. If you need more whites or yolks, use an additional bowl to keep the successful white or yolks while you continue separating the rest. Avoid separating an egg over the bowl of ingredients, just in case the yolk breaks and mixes with the white—that can mess up your recipe!

Tempering Eggs

When adding warm liquid to eggs, you'll need to "temper" the eggs. Tempering eggs means to raise the temperature of beaten eggs so they don't curdle (cook) when warm ingredients are added. You don't want pieces of scrambled eggs in your baked goods! To temper your eggs, slowly add the warm liquid to the beaten eggs in a bowl while stirring or whisking continuously.

LESSON 2 RECIPE TUTORIAL
little meringue clouds

PREP TIME: 15 minutes

COOK TIME: 2 hours (plus 2 hours left in oven)

YIELD: 24 clouds

TOOLS/EQUIPMENT

- 2 baking sheets
- Parchment paper
- Stand mixer (or hand mixer and a large bowl)

4 large egg whites, at room temperature
½ teaspoon cream of tartar
¼ teaspoon table salt
1 cup confectioners' sugar

 TROUBLESHOOTING TIP:
If your meringues turned brown, use an oven thermometer to double-check that your oven temperature is correct. If it's off, you may need to reduce your cooking temperature next time and peek through with the oven light on to keep an eye on things.

Preheat the oven to 200˚F.
But first, move one oven rack to the upper third of the oven, and the other to the lower third. Line 2 baking sheets with parchment paper.

Beat the egg whites.
In a bowl, add the egg whites, cream of tartar, and salt. With a mixer, blend on medium until the whites start getting foamy, 1 to 2 minutes. Increase the speed to medium-high and continue beating until the egg whites become thick and opaque, 1 to 2 additional minutes.

Add the sugar.
With the mixer on medium-high, slowly add the confectioners' sugar to the bowl, about 1 tablespoon at a time. Continue beating until the egg whites are shiny and stiff peaks form, 4 to 6 minutes.

Bake the meringues.
Using a small spoon, transfer little mounds of the egg white mixture onto the baking sheets, leaving about 2 inches between clouds. Using the back of a spoon, shape meringues into little clouds by making indentations and peaks into meringues. Bake for 2 hours. Turn the oven off and let the clouds remain in the oven for an additional 1 to 2 hours, or until dry and crispy.

MIXING AND FOLDING

There are many ways to combine ingredients, including mixing, beating, creaming, folding, and more. Does it really matter which you use? Well, sometimes it does and sometimes it doesn't. When in doubt, follow the recipe before experimenting with something different.

Following Mixing Instructions

When it comes to mixing, a good rule of thumb is to follow a recipe exactly the first time. The second time, you might choose to experiment a little so you can compare your results to the first time. Here are some basic mixing terms:

Beat: Combining the ingredients using a stand or electric hand mixer, or whisking by hand until well combined.

Cream: Some recipes will call for "creaming" the butter and sugar together. Creaming is combining a fat such as butter or shortening with sugar. It helps give structure to baked goods such as cakes, cookies, and pastries and helps them rise. It's easiest to do this with a stand mixer or electric hand mixer.

Fold: Folding is used for delicate ingredients, when you don't want to deflate air already whipped into the ingredients. See a detailed explanation of how to fold on the next page.

Stir: Stirring is a general term for hand-mixing ingredients, best done with a spoon or rubber spatula. It's a good and simple technique when you don't need to incorporate air into the ingredients.

Whip: Whipping is used for things such as cream and egg whites, when you want to add air into the ingredient(s). It's usually easiest to use a stand mixer or electric hand mixer, but you can also use a whisk for whipping. You may see the terms soft, medium, or stiff/firm peaks when whipping cream or egg whites. With whipping, when you stop beating and hold the beater upside down, soft peaks will flop over, medium peaks will hold their shape but curl a bit at the tip, and stiff/firm peaks will stand straight up.

Mixing Wet and Dry Ingredients Separately

For some baked goods, such as muffins and quick breads, you should mix the wet and dry ingredients separately before combining. In one bowl, mix together the wet ingredients until well combined. In another bowl, place the dry ingredients (see image A). Mix them until the ingredients are evenly spread out. Push the dry ingredients to the sides of the bowl to make a "well," and pour the wet ingredients into the middle (see image B). Mix the dry and wet ingredients together until just combined, being careful not to overmix (see image C).

Overmixing can cause:

- some baked goods, such as cookies, to over-aerate, which means they will rise then collapse when baked.

- too much gluten development. Too much gluten can cause cookies, muffins, cakes, and breads to be tough and chewier than you want.

- cold butter and shortening bits to become too small and warm, causing pastries, biscuits, scones, and pie dough to be less tender and flaky.

To avoid overmixing, combine ingredients until they are just mixed together and no streaks of ingredients remain, unless your recipe directs you otherwise. Do the minimum amount of mixing to blend ingredients, and don't continue mixing for long periods of time unless instructed to do so. For some baked goods such as muffins and quick breads, lumps in the batter are okay, even good.

Folding

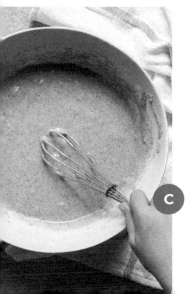

Sometimes, delicate ingredients such as whipped egg whites or whipped cream must be "folded" into other ingredients. Folding is used to carefully combine ingredients without removing the air from the mixture. Rubber spatulas and large spoons are generally best for folding. With a gentle hand, add the lighter mixture (such as the whipped egg whites or cream) into the heavier mixture (such as cooled melted chocolate). Gently run the spatula or spoon around the side of the bowl, then along the bottom of the bowl, then fold the mixture onto itself. Rotate the bowl about 90 degrees, and repeat until the ingredients are just combined.

LESSON 3 RECIPE TUTORIAL
cinnamon buttermilk muffins

PREP TIME: 20 minutes

COOK TIME: 25 minutes

YIELD: 12 muffins

TOOLS/EQUIPMENT

- Muffin pan
- Paper liners (optional)
- 2 medium bowls
- Whisk
- Wire rack

FOR THE MUFFINS

Butter, for greasing the pan
(optional)

Flour, for dusting the pan
(optional)

2½ cups all-purpose flour

1 cup granulated sugar

2 teaspoons baking soda

1 teaspoon cinnamon plus
½ teaspoon cinnamon, divided

½ teaspoon table salt

¾ cup buttermilk

½ cup vegetable or canola oil

3 large eggs, at room temperature

2 teaspoons vanilla extract

FOR THE TOPPING

2 tablespoons granulated sugar

½ teaspoon cinnamon

Preheat the oven to 375˚F.
Grease and lightly flour a 12-cup muffin pan, or line with paper liners.

Mix the dry ingredients.
In a medium bowl, stir together the flour, 1 cup of granulated sugar, baking soda, 1 teaspoon cinnamon, and salt.

Mix the wet ingredients.
In another medium bowl, whisk together the buttermilk, oil, eggs, and vanilla until well blended.

Combine the ingredients.
Make a well in the dry mixture, and then pour the wet mixture into the middle. Mix until just combined. Some small lumps are okay.

Make the topping.
In a small bowl, mix together the 2 tablespoons granulated sugar and the remaining ½ teaspoon cinnamon until blended.

Bake the muffins.
Spoon the batter into the muffin cups about ⅔ full. Sprinkle the cinnamon sugar topping on top. Bake for 20 to 25 minutes, or until a toothpick inserted into the middle of a muffin comes out clean. Cool slightly, then remove the muffins from the pan and cool on a wire rack.

TRY INSTEAD: For a crunchier topping, substitute an equal amount of turbinado sugar in the topping for the granulated sugar.

LESSON 4

CREAMING BUTTER AND SUGAR

Learning how to cream butter and sugar will help you produce delicious baked goods. Creaming is combining a fat (such as butter or shortening) with sugar. Creaming helps baked goods rise, resulting in a light, fluffy texture.

Using an Electric Mixer

The best way to cream butter (or shortening) and sugar is to use a stand mixer or electric hand mixer. Here's how: Place room-temperature butter in a bowl, and beat on low speed until the butter is smooth, 10 to 20 seconds. Slowly add the sugar, and beat on medium speed. Scrape the sides of the bowl with a rubber spatula as needed to make sure everything is well mixed. It should take 2 to 5 minutes of beating to get the right texture. The butter and sugar mixture should be a pale yellow color, fluffy and smooth.

Getting the Right Texture

When creaming butter and sugar, it's important to start with room-temperature butter to achieve the right texture. Butter should be left on the counter for at least a half hour or until soft before you start. You can tell it's ready if when you press a finger on the butter, it leaves a small indentation. Some microwaves also have a "soften" setting for butter, but be careful using it so you don't end up with melted butter and have to start over!

IS IT DONE YET? HOW TO TELL

You can check your baked goods for doneness by using some tests and even just looking. Your oven, altitude, and humidity can all affect baking time and results. Use your best judgment, but always check for doneness on the earlier side specified in the recipe, or even a few minutes before.

CAKES AND CUPCAKES

Insert a toothpick into the center of the cake. If it's done, the toothpick should come out clean or with a few crumbs. If there is liquid batter on the toothpick, continue baking a few minutes more.

A cooked cake usually has a golden-brown surface and edges, and the edges pull away from the sides of the pan. If you gently touch the cake in the center, the cake should spring back.

PIES AND TARTS

The crust should look golden brown and toasted.

Fruit pies should be bubbling in the center. I also like to use a toothpick and test the doneness of the fruit in pies like apple and pear. Fruit should be soft in the center.

Other pies, such as pumpkin, may appear slightly jiggly or undercooked in the center, but will firm up or "set" once cooled.

BREAD

Yeast breads should have a golden-brown crust and be pulling away from the sides of the pan. If you gently tap on it, it should make a hollow sound.

Quick breads (no yeast) should be golden brown and slightly darker around the edges, and be pulling away from the sides of the pan. If done, a toothpick or wooden skewer inserted into the middle will come out clean or with a few crumbs.

COOKIES

Fully baked cookies will be golden brown on the bottom when lifted gently with a spatula. Cookies actually continue cooking slightly after being removed from the oven, so try to remove them from the oven a bit on the earlier side, before they get overcooked.

vanilla cupcakes
WITH CHOCOLATE FUDGE FROSTING

PREP TIME: 30 minutes

COOK TIME: 25 minutes

YIELD: 12 cupcakes

TOOLS/EQUIPMENT

- Muffin pan
- Stand mixer (or hand mixer and large bowl)
- Medium bowl
- Paper liners (optional)

FOR THE CAKE

Butter, for greasing the pan (optional)

Flour, for dusting the pan (optional)

1 cup all-purpose flour

1 teaspoon baking powder

¼ teaspoon baking soda

¼ teaspoon table salt

⅓ cup unsalted butter, at room temperature

⅔ cup granulated sugar

1½ teaspoons vanilla extract

2 large eggs, at room temperature

⅓ cup milk (2 percent or whole)

FOR THE FROSTING

⅓ cup unsalted butter

⅔ cup unsweetened cocoa powder

3 cups confectioners' sugar

⅓ cup milk (2 percent or whole)

1 teaspoon vanilla extract

Preheat the oven to 350˚F.

Grease and lightly flour a 12-cup muffin pan or line with paper liners.

Mix the dry ingredients.

In a medium bowl, stir together the flour, baking powder, baking soda, and salt.

Cream the butter and sugar.

In a large bowl, beat the ⅓ cup butter with an electric mixer on medium speed for about 10 seconds, or until smooth. Beat in the granulated sugar and 1½ teaspoons of vanilla until well blended and light and fluffy, about 2 minutes. Beat in the eggs, one at a time, beating after each egg is added.

Combine the cake ingredients.

Alternate adding the flour mixture and the ⅓ cup milk to the butter mixture, beating on low after adding each, until the batter is just combined.

Bake the cupcakes.

Spoon the batter into muffin cups about ½ full. Bake for 18 to 20 minutes, or until a toothpick inserted into the center comes out clean. Cool slightly, then transfer to a wire rack to finish cooling. »

Make the frosting.

In a small saucepan over medium heat, melt the remaining ⅓ cup butter. Add the cocoa powder and bring to a boil, stirring constantly. Pour the mixture into a medium bowl and cool completely. Beat in the confectioners' sugar with the electric mixer on medium speed. Beat in the ⅓ cup milk, a little at a time, until the frosting is a smooth, spreadable consistency, then beat in 1 teaspoon of vanilla.

Frost the cupcakes.

When cupcakes are completely cooled, frost with a spatula.

HELPFUL HINT: If the frosting seems too dry, add a little more milk and continue beating. If frosting appears too thin, stir in a little more confectioners' sugar.

DID YOU KNOW? Letting your eggs stand at room temperature for 30 minutes before using provides more volume to baked goods.

HOW TO FROST AND DECORATE

Frosting and decorating cakes and cupcakes can be a lot of fun, because you can use your imagination and be infinitely creative! But for starters, the easiest way to frost a cake or cupcake is with a butter knife. Scoop some frosting onto a cooled cake or cupcake and use your spatula or knife to cover the surface. Frosting a still-warm cake can result in excess crumbs or melted frosting.

Fondant—a thick paste resembling icing—as well as piping bags and tips are fun tools for decorating cakes and cupcakes. These techniques take some practice, but there are many great videos and tutorials on the Internet to help you get started with both methods.

You don't need to spend a lot of time decorating to get a wonderful result. You probably have some great toppings already sitting in your kitchen. Here are some fun items to use to decorate your cakes and cupcakes:

- Animal crackers
- Candy
- Cereal
- Chocolate chips
- Cookies
- Fruit
- Graham crackers, crushed
- Ice cream cones, crushed
- Mini marshmallows
- Melted chocolate
- Nuts, chopped
- Sprinkles

MAKING DOUGH

Pie and pastry dough can be very delicate to work with. When I was younger, I had the hardest time getting my pie crusts to taste good, look pretty, and not fall down the sides of the pan when baked. It can take some time and practice to get the hang of it, but once you get there, you'll be so proud of your masterpiece!

Cutting in Butter

For pie dough and other baked goods like biscuits and scones, you'll first want to learn how to cut in the butter. "Cutting in" is combining butter or another fat with flour. You can use a pastry cutter, the back of a fork, or two knives for this process. Start cutting cold butter into small cubes and place them over the flour. Using one of the mentioned tools, crush or cut the butter into the flour until the mixture is crumbly and reduced to small pea-size bits. Having small bits of butter or other fat will create small air pockets in the dough. This is what makes pastry light and flaky. Be careful to not overmix and overwork the dough, or you won't get those nice pockets of air and flaky crust.

You can also cut in butter using a food processor! Place a steel blade in the food processor bowl. Add the flour, salt, butter, and shortening, and pulse the food processor again and again until pea-size crumbs form. With the food processor running, slowly add the water, 1 tablespoon at a time, through the feed tube at the top until a dough forms.

KID CHEF TIP: Protect your oven from overflow! Even as an adult, I'm still learning and making mistakes. One time, I had a pie overflow so badly in the oven it made a huge mess! Now I always try to place my pies on rimmed baking sheets just in case.

Rolling Dough

Once your dough is combined, for pastry and pie crusts you'll want to refrigerate the dough to allow the butter to get cold again, about 30 to 45 minutes. Form the dough into a thick disk and wrap it tightly in plastic wrap before placing in the refrigerator.

After the dough has chilled, unwrap it and place it on a floured surface. Use a heavy rolling pin to roll out the dough to fit the pan you're planning to use, or to the thickness directed in the recipe. If the dough is sticky, it's helpful to flour the rolling pin and your hands.

Gently roll dough from the inside out, without creating holes in the dough. If your dough gets too soft, place it back in the fridge for 10 to 20 minutes or until cold and firm.

Pie crusts should be thin and even in thickness throughout. When you have the dough rolled out enough, roll the dough around your rolling pin, then transfer the dough to the pan, unrolling it over the pan.

Tips for Baking Crusts

Pies can be single crust or double crust. Either way, it's best for the dough to be as cold as possible before filling and baking. The cold butter and/or shortening help form thin layers in the dough. When the fat melts in the oven, it helps create flakiness in the crust.

For single-crust pies that do not require the filling to be baked, you'll need to "blind bake" the crust. Once your crust is in the pan and your edges fluted (see Pie Fluting: How To, below), use a fork to prick the bottom and sides of the pie crust to keep it from bubbling up while baking. You can also use dried beans to keep the pie crust put while baking—they even sell "pie beads," which are weighted beads designed to hold crusts in place as they bake!

For double-crust pies with a filling, cut some slits in the top crust so steam can escape from the filling. You can also cut out decorative shapes, like hearts or apple shapes—use a cookie cutter if you wish!

PIE FLUTING: HOW TO

Fluting, which is the art of pressing a pattern around the top edge of a pie crust before it is baked, has good reason for being there. For single-crust pies, it helps prevent the crust from sliding down the side of the pan when baked. For double-crusted pies, it helps seal the filling inside.

To flute a crust, using a knife or kitchen scissors, trim the edge of the dough to about an inch over the edge of the pan. Take the edging and roll it under itself, which will give you a thicker edge to work with. Place a hand on either side of the dough. Use the pointer finger of your inside hand to push the dough between the thumb and pointer finger of your other hand to form a U or V shape. Continue your pattern all around the edge of the pie.

LESSON 5 RECIPE TUTORIAL
pie dough

PREP TIME: 10 minutes (plus 30 minutes chill time)

COOK TIME: None (until used in a recipe)

YIELD: 1 pie crust

TOOLS/EQUIPMENT

- Medium bowl
- Pastry cutter (or fork or two knives; see Cutting in Butter, page 42)
- Plastic wrap

1⅓ cups all-purpose flour

½ teaspoon table salt

4 tablespoons cold unsalted butter, cubed

¼ cup shortening

3 to 6 tablespoons ice cold water

Mix the dry ingredients.

In a medium bowl, stir together the flour and salt.

Cut in the fats.

Add the butter and shortening to the dry ingredients. Using a pastry cutter (or the back of a fork or two knives), cut in the butter and shortening until pea-size crumbs of dough form.

Add the water.

Add the water, 1 tablespoon at a time, to the dough. Stir and repeat just until a soft dough forms. Form the dough into a ball.

Refrigerate the dough.

Place the ball of dough on a large piece of plastic wrap. Flatten the dough into a thick disk, then cover with plastic wrap and refrigerate for at least 30 minutes before rolling out.

> HELPFUL HINT: This dough can be used in a variety of recipes, including Homemade PB&J Breakfast Tarts (page 162), Mini Blueberry Peach Crostatas (page 168), and Southern Chocolate Walnut Pie (page 160).

> TRY INSTEAD: Add a dash of your favorite spice like cinnamon or a little citrus zest for a fun-flavored pie crust.

YEAST DOUGH

Working with yeast can be a little intimidating—after all, it's a living organism, and like anything living, it has its preferences! But when you learn the art of working with yeast, you can create delicious pizza crusts, breads, and other treats. Don't worry if the first few times you work with yeast, things don't work. It may take a little experimenting with, just like other baking techniques.

Water Temperature

Using the correct temperature of water in yeast doughs is really important. The water should be warm, but not too hot and not too cold. If your water and resulting dough are too hot, you can kill the yeast and your dough will not rise. If your water is too cold, the yeast will not be activated and your dough will also not rise. Most bakers will recommend your water to be between 95°F and 130°F. I usually aim for about 110°F.

If you are unsure how warm your water is, you can buy an inexpensive thermometer and try it out until you get used to feeling the different temperatures of water before making your dough.

Kneading

Once you combine all your dough ingredients, kneading is generally necessary. Kneading, or massaging and squeezing, dough allows the protein gluten to form, which gives bread its texture. There are different methods of kneading:

- **By hand.** Place the dough on a floured surface. Press down firmly on the dough then stretch it with the heel of your hand. Fold the dough over, rotate the dough 90 degrees, and repeat. This is a good workout!

- **Stand mixer.** A stand mixer with a dough hook can make kneading easy and hands-free, since you can let the mixer do all the work.

- **Bread machine.** Some bread machines can mix the ingredients *and* knead the dough for you; or just have it do the kneading for another hands-free option.

YEAST: A LIVING ORGANISM!

Ever wonder what yeast is? Yeast is actually a single-celled organism. But don't worry, it's perfectly safe to bake with and eat! Yeast cells are so small that it takes about 20 billion yeast cells just to weigh one gram.

Yeast is needed in many doughs to make them rise and create a light airy texture. There are different types of yeast, such as compressed cake yeast (also known as fresh yeast), active dry yeast, quick-rise yeast, and instant yeast. We will be using active dry yeast in this book. Active dry yeast is found in small packets, usually in the baking aisle of the grocery store.

Yeast gets its energy from its favorite food source: sugar and other sweeteners. When the yeast eats sugar, it starts a process of fermentation, which converts the sugar to alcohol and carbon dioxide. This allows the dough to rise and create air pockets. The yeast eventually dies off when you bake the dough, and the alcohol evaporates.

YEAST CAN BE TRICKY!

I still sometimes have a hard time getting my water temperature exactly right when working with yeast. If the water is not warm enough, the yeast will not activate and you'll have flat bread. If the water is too hot, you'll kill the yeast and end up with a flat, tough dough. Even when testing recipes for this book, all my dough came out great except for the one for the Honey Oat Bread (page 80). I was in a hurry and since everything else turned out fine, I wasn't careful and used water that was too hot. The dough was tough and hard, so I had to start over!

Dough is typically kneaded until it is elastic and smooth. Then it is placed in an oiled bowl (see image A, page 48), covered, and allowed to rise and "proof." Read on to learn about rising and proofing, and why it's so important to the baking process.

Rising and Proofing

Dough needs the chance to rise, because the yeast ferments, creating carbon dioxide, which allows air to develop inside the dough. This is what gives breads and other baked goods their volume and airiness. In fact, you'll often see recipes that call for allowing the dough to rise twice.

A

B

The second rise helps you get a finer crumb and avoid giant air holes in your bread.

Most recipes will tell you to cover the dough with a towel or plastic wrap, and let it rise in a dark, warm place. The humidity and temperature of homes can vary, so results will vary. But generally, if you cover your dough with a towel and place it in a dark corner, perhaps in a cabinet, you'll get the results you want (see image "B").

After the dough has risen once, your recipe may direct you to "punch down" your dough, reshape it, and let it rise again. Punching down helps remove extra gas bubbles from the dough, and results in a finer grain. The process of punching down and reshaping also moves the yeast and moisture around, allowing it to ferment other areas of the dough.

Proofing is the final rise before baking. Professional bakers may use a proof box, which is a large cabinet that holds the air temperature between 80°F and 90°F and humidity at about 75 percent. But for the rest of us who don't have such equipment, here are a few popular home methods for proofing dough:

- **Boiling water.** Adjust the racks in your oven to a lower and middle position, but leave the oven turned off. Place a cake pan or 9-by-13-inch baking pan on the bottom rack. Carefully pour about 3 cups of boiling water into the pan—have an adult help if this is new or uncomfortable to you. Place your dough in the covered bowl on the middle rack, above the pan with the water. Close the oven door and let the dough rise as directed in the recipe.

STORING BAKED GOODS

If you're lucky enough to have any left-overs, let's talk about storage. For different baked goods, there are different ways to store them for freshness. If you want to store baked goods for longer than a few days, most can be wrapped tightly, then placed in an airtight bag or container and frozen.

Yeast breads. Store crusty breads made with yeast at room temperature in a bag with a little air. An airtight bag will make the crust soggy. This bread will usually stay good for about three to four days.

Cakes, cookies, and muffins. Baked good-ies such as brownies, cookies, muffins, quick breads, cakes, and cupcakes can be covered and stored at room temperature. They may start to taste a little stale after about two days, but can usually be eaten for about a week.

Non-dairy pies. Non-dairy pies can be stored covered at room temperature. Although they're best if eaten within a few days, non-dairy pies are good for about a week. However, the crust may become soggy and the taste may diminish after a day or two.

Cheesecakes and dairy baked goods. Cheesecakes, cream pies, and other baked goods with dairy, such as dairy-based frostings with butter, cream cheese, or cream, should be stored in the fridge. These baked goods usually stay good for about a week, but for best taste and texture, bring them to room temperature before serving.

- **Oven.** Preheat your oven to 200°F. Once preheated, turn the oven off. Place your dough in a covered bowl on the middle rack of the oven and let it rise. The oven will remain warm for a while, allowing your dough to rise. However, if your oven is too warm, your dough may become crispy around the edges.

- **Countertop.** Some people simply like to leave their dough in a covered bowl right on the countertop, away from windows and drafts. Results can vary, depending on how warm and humid your home is.

Once your dough is ready for the oven, remember to remove the cover (plastic wrap, towel, etc.) before baking!

LESSON 6 RECIPE TUTORIAL
homemade pizza dough

PREP TIME: 20 minutes (plus 1 hour for dough to rise)

COOK TIME: None (until used in a recipe)

YIELD: About 1 large pizza

TOOLS/EQUIPMENT

- Large bowl
- Stand mixer with hook attachment (or wooden spoon)
- Plastic wrap

2¾ to 3¼ cups all-purpose flour

1 (¼-ounce) envelope active dry yeast

1 teaspoon sugar

1 teaspoon table salt

1 cup warm water (105°F to 115°F)

3 tablespoons olive oil, divided

Flour, for dusting the work surface

Combine the dry ingredients.
In a large bowl, add 2¾ cups of flour and the yeast, sugar, and salt.

Add the liquid.
Add the water and 2 tablespoons of olive oil to the bowl. Beat with a stand mixer with a hook attachment or a wooden spoon until the dough forms a soft ball. Mix in additional flour as needed.

Knead the dough.
Place the dough onto a lightly floured surface and knead until the dough is smooth and elastic, 6 to 8 minutes.

Let the dough rest.
Grease a large bowl with the remaining table-spoon of oil, add the dough, turn to coat, cover with plastic wrap and place in a warm, draft-free place to double in size, about 1 hour.

> **TROUBLESHOOTING TIP:** If the dough is sticky, add more flour, 1 tablespoon at a time. If the dough is too dry, add more warm water, 1 tablespoon at a time.

> **PRO TIP:** To transform this crust into a pizza, roll out the crust thinly on a floured surface, transfer to a nonstick baking sheet, then top with desired toppings. Bake at 400°F until the cheese is melted and the crust is golden brown, about 10 minutes.

MELTING CHOCOLATE

Mmm . . . just the idea of warm, gooey melted chocolate can make you hungry! Delicious by itself, melted chocolate also comes in handy for many baking applications, including brownies, frostings, drizzling over cookies, and more. The secret to perfect melted chocolate is to take your time and use care in melting it. The slightest bit of water or steam can cause chocolate to "seize," turning it clumpy and dull. Chocolate can also burn easily. To melt chocolate, you can either use a double boiler or make your own melting vessel. Both methods will warm your chocolate to a smooth and creamy consistency.

Using a Double Boiler

A double boiler is a tool that consists of two pots: a large saucepan, and a smaller saucepan, which fits snugly on top of the larger one. To use a double boiler, fill the bottom pan with an inch or two of water, and set the smaller pan on top. Place the pans on the stovetop over medium-high heat. When the water begins to boil, reduce the heat to low. Place your

MICROWAVING CHOCOLATE: IT CAN BE DONE!

The safest way to melt chocolate is in a double boiler. However, you might be in a hurry or want to experiment a little more, so you're probably curious about using a microwave to melt chocolate. You can melt chocolate in the microwave; however, microwaves vary. You'll need to practice and see what works the best with your microwave.

To melt chocolate in the microwave, place the chocolate in a wide, shallow, microwave-safe bowl. It's best if the chocolate pieces are all about the same size, so cut large bars of chocolate into small pieces.

Place the bowl in the microwave, and heat the chocolate for 15 to 20 seconds on low to medium power. Remove the chocolate from the microwave, and stir. Repeat, heating the chocolate for 15- to 20-second intervals, stirring well after each cook time, until the chocolate is smooth. The heat in the bowl will help melt the chocolate more as you're stirring.

chocolate in the top pan and stir constantly until the chocolate is melted and smooth (see image A).

The steam from the water below will slowly heat the upper saucepan, letting the chocolate melt slowly, consistently, and smoothly. Too high of heat can cause the chocolate to burn or seize, so a double boiler offers a safe way to melt chocolate without complications.

If your pan is starting to cool down, check to make sure the water hasn't all evaporated from the bottom pan, and add more water if necessary. Be careful not to get any steam or water into the chocolate.

Make Your Own Double Boiler

You can easily make your own double boiler using a saucepan and a heat-proof bowl.

Fill a small to medium saucepan with an inch or two of water. Heat the water to a boil, then reduce the heat to low. Gently place a heat-proof bowl on top of the saucepan. Stainless steel bowls work well for this. The bowl should be completely dry. Make sure the bowl fits snugly over the bottom pan so that steam doesn't escape from the pan below and cause your chocolate to seize. The bowl should not be touching the water.

Just like with a double boiler, fill the bowl with your chocolate, and stir continuously until the chocolate is melted and smooth (see image B). Now it's ready to use for spreading or dipping!

Bars of Chocolate

Bars and blocks of chocolate work well for melting; often better than chocolate chips. If using a bar or block, first cut the chocolate into uniform-size chunks. A serrated (jagged-edged) knife works well for cutting chocolate. High-quality semisweet, bittersweet, and unsweetened chocolate are common types of chocolate that often come in bars or blocks.

LESSON 7 RECIPE TUTORIAL
brownie bites

PREP TIME: 30 minutes

COOK TIME: 20 minutes

YIELD: 24 brownie bites

TOOLS/EQUIPMENT

- Mini muffin pan
- Hand mixer
- Mini paper liners (optional)
- Small bowl
- Medium bowl

Butter, for greasing the pan (optional)

½ cup (1 stick) unsalted butter

1 cup semisweet chocolate chips

¼ cup plus 2 tablespoons all-purpose flour

¾ teaspoon baking powder

¼ teaspoon table salt

2 large eggs, at room temperature

½ cup granulated sugar

1 teaspoon vanilla extract

Preheat the oven to 350˚F.

Grease a mini muffin pan or line with mini paper liners.

Melt the chocolate.

In the top of a double boiler, add the butter and chocolate chips. Place over boiling water, then reduce the heat to low. Stir constantly, until the chocolate and butter are melted and smooth. Remove from heat and cool completely.

Mix the dry ingredients.

In a small bowl, mix together the flour, baking powder, and salt until blended.

Mix the eggs and sugar.

In a medium bowl, mix together the eggs and sugar with a whisk or an electric mixer on medium speed until well blended. Beat in the vanilla. Beat in the cooled melted chocolate, then mix in the dry ingredients until just combined.

Bake the brownies.

Spoon the brownie batter into mini muffin cups, about ¾ full. Bake for 15 to 20 minutes, or until a toothpick inserted into the middle comes out clean. Cool brownies completely, then remove from the pan.

TRY INSTEAD: For a deeper chocolate flavor, you can substitute dark chocolate chips for the semisweet chocolate chips.

PART TWO
recipes

3

muffins & breads

mini triple chocolate muffins

PREP TIME: 20 minutes

COOK TIME: 12 minutes

YIELD: 24 mini muffins

TOOLS/EQUIPMENT

- Mini muffin pan
- Paper liners (optional)
- 2 medium bowls
- Wire rack

Butter, for greasing the pan (optional)

Flour, for dusting the pan (optional)

1¼ cups all-purpose flour

½ cup brown sugar

½ cup unsweetened cocoa powder

½ teaspoon table salt

½ teaspoon baking powder

½ teaspoon baking soda

¾ cup milk (2 percent or whole)

⅓ cup vegetable or canola oil

2 large eggs, at room temperature

2 teaspoons vanilla extract

¼ cup finely chopped semisweet chocolate

¼ cup finely chopped white chocolate

Preheat the oven to 375°F.

Grease and lightly flour a 24-cup mini muffin pan or line with paper liners.

Mix the dry ingredients.

In a medium bowl, stir together the flour, brown sugar, cocoa powder, salt, baking powder, and baking soda.

Mix the wet ingredients.

In another bowl, stir together the milk, oil, eggs, and vanilla until well blended.

Blend the ingredients.

Make a well in the middle of the dry ingredients, then pour the wet ingredients in the middle and stir to mix. When almost blended, add the semi-sweet and white chocolate, and mix until just combined. Some small lumps are okay.

Bake the muffins.

Spoon the batter into the muffin cups about ⅔ full. Bake for 8 to 12 minutes, or until a toothpick inserted into the middle of a muffin comes out clean. Cool slightly, then transfer the muffins to a wire rack to cool.

> TRY INSTEAD: Instead of chopped semisweet chocolate and white chocolate, you can use chopped nuts, toffee chips, or your favorite baking chips.

cherry orange scones

PREP TIME: 20 minutes

COOK TIME: 20 minutes

YIELD: 8 scones

TOOLS/EQUIPMENT

- Baking sheet
- Parchment paper (optional)
- Large bowl
- Zester
- Pastry cutter (or fork or two knives; see Cutting in Butter, page 42)
- Pastry brush
- Small bowl
- Whisk (or fork)

FOR THE SCONES

Butter, for greasing the baking sheet (optional)

Flour, for the work surface

2 cups all-purpose flour

2 tablespoons granulated sugar

1 tablespoon baking powder

1 teaspoon table salt

1 teaspoon freshly grated orange zest

5 tablespoons cold unsalted butter, cut into cubes

¾ cup dried cherries, chopped

1 cup plus 2 tablespoons heavy whipping cream, divided

FOR THE GLAZE

½ cup confectioners' sugar

2 tablespoons freshly squeezed orange juice

Preheat the oven to 400°F.

Grease a baking sheet or line with parchment paper.

Mix the dry ingredients.

In a large bowl, mix together the flour, granulated sugar, baking powder, salt, and orange zest.

Cut in the butter.

Using a pastry cutter, cut in the butter until the flour mixture is coarse pea-size crumbs. Stir in the dried cherries.

Combine the ingredients.

Make a well in the center of the dry ingredients. Pour 1 cup of cream into the middle and stir until just combined.

Form the scones.

Divide the dough in half. Place each half on a lightly floured surface and form each half into a circle about 1¼ inch thick. Cut each circle in half, and then in half again, forming 8 triangles between the two rounds.

Bake the scones.

Place the scones on the prepared baking sheet. Brush the tops of the scones with the remaining 2 tablespoons of cream. Bake for 15 to 20 minutes or until golden brown around the edges. Cool slightly.

Make the glaze.

In a small bowl, whisk together the confectioners' sugar and orange juice until thin and smooth. Brush over the scones.

NUT-FREE

blueberry muffin tops
WITH CHEESECAKE DRIZZLE

PREP TIME: 15 minutes
COOK TIME: 14 minutes
YIELD: 24 muffin tops

TOOLS/EQUIPMENT
- 2 baking sheets
- Parchment paper (optional)
- 2 medium bowls
- Whisk
- Small bowl
- Wire rack

FOR THE MUFFIN TOPS
Butter, for greasing the baking sheets (optional)
1½ cups all-purpose flour
¾ cup granulated sugar
1½ teaspoons baking powder
½ teaspoon table salt
⅓ cup milk (2 percent or whole)
⅓ cup vegetable or canola oil
1 large egg plus 1 large egg yolk
1 teaspoon vanilla extract
2 cups fresh blueberries

FOR THE CHEESECAKE DRIZZLE
4 ounces cream cheese, at room temperature
½ cup confectioners' sugar
¼ teaspoon vanilla extract
3 to 5 tablespoons milk (2 percent or whole)

Preheat the oven to 375°F.
Grease 2 large baking sheets, or line with parchment paper.

Mix the dry ingredients.
In a medium bowl, stir together the flour, granulated sugar, baking powder, and salt.

Mix the wet ingredients.
In another medium bowl, whisk together the ⅓ cup of milk, oil, egg and egg yolk, and 1 teaspoon vanilla until well combined.

Combine the ingredients.
Make a well in the center of the dry ingredients. Add the wet ingredients to the middle of the dry ingredients, and stir until nearly blended. Some lumps are okay. Gently fold in the blueberries until everything is just combined.

Bake the muffins.
Using a large ice cream scoop or spoon, spoon about 3 tablespoons of the batter onto the prepared pans for each top, leaving about 2 inches of room between each. Bake for 10 to 14 minutes, or until a toothpick inserted into the middle comes out clean and muffins are slightly browned around edges. Cool slightly, then remove muffins from the pans and cool on a wire rack. »

Make the drizzle.

Meanwhile, in a small bowl, mix together the cream cheese, confectioners' sugar, and ¼ teaspoon of vanilla. Slowly stir in the milk, a little at a time, until well blended and a thin consistency. With a fork, drizzle over the cooled muffins.

TRY INSTEAD: For a crunchy muffin topping, sprinkle the tops of the muffins with turbinado sugar.

TROUBLESHOOTING TIP: If your muffins stick to the pan, run a butter knife around the edges to loosen.

HELPFUL HINT: I tested making these muffin tops three ways: on baking sheets, in greased and floured muffin tins, and in muffins tins with paper liners. All three methods worked well but had slightly different results. I liked the large muffin tops that the baking sheets made, but the lightly greased and floured muffin tins made great golden-brown tops, and of course using a pan with paper liners is an easy option with less cleanup!

cornbread muffins
WITH ORANGE HONEY BUTTER

PREP TIME: 10 minutes
COOK TIME: 17 minutes
YIELD: 18 muffins

TOOLS/EQUIPMENT
- 2 muffin pans
- Paper liners (optional)
- Large bowl
- Medium bowl
- Zester
- Small bowl

FOR THE MUFFINS
Butter, for greasing the pans (optional)
Flour, for dusting the pans (optional)
1 cup all-purpose flour
1 cup yellow cornmeal
½ cup granulated sugar
1 tablespoon baking powder
1 teaspoon table salt
1 cup milk (2 percent or whole)
½ cup (1 stick) unsalted butter, melted and cooled
¼ cup honey
2 large eggs, at room temperature

FOR THE ORANGE HONEY BUTTER
½ cup (1 stick) unsalted butter, at room temperature
¼ teaspoon table salt
2 tablespoons honey
1 teaspoon freshly grated orange zest
1 teaspoon freshly squeezed orange juice

Preheat the oven to 400°F.
Generously grease and lightly flour 18 cups of 2 (12-cup) muffin pans, or line the pans with paper liners.

Mix the dry ingredients.
In a large bowl, mix together the flour, cornmeal, sugar, baking powder, and 1 teaspoon of salt.

Mix the wet ingredients.
In a medium bowl, mix together the milk, ½ cup of melted butter, ¼ cup of honey, and the eggs until well combined.

Blend the ingredients.
Make a well in the middle of the dry ingredients, and pour the wet ingredients into the middle. Mix until just combined.

Bake the muffins.
Spoon the batter into the prepared pans. Bake for 14 to 17 minutes or until a toothpick inserted into the middle of a muffin comes out clean.

Make the orange honey butter.
Meanwhile, in a small bowl, mix together the ½ cup of room-temperature butter, ¼ teaspoon of salt, 2 tablespoons of honey, orange zest, and orange juice until well combined. Serve with the warm muffins.

TRY INSTEAD: Instead of orange zest and orange juice, you can mix in a little of your favorite jam or jelly.

sticky monkey bread bites

PREP TIME: 40 minutes (plus 2 hours for dough to rise)
COOK TIME: 20 minutes
YIELD: 18 bites

TOOLS/EQUIPMENT

- 2 muffin pans
- Paper liners (optional)
- Stand mixer or large bowl
- 2 small bowls

FOR THE DOUGH

1 cup warm milk (2 percent or whole, 105 to 115°F)
2 tablespoons granulated sugar
1 (¼-ounce) envelope active dry yeast
2 tablespoons butter, at room temperature, plus additional for greasing the pans
3 to 4 cups all-purpose flour
½ teaspoon table salt
1 large egg
1 tablespoon vegetable or canola oil

FOR THE TOPPING

½ cup (1 stick) unsalted butter, melted
1 cup brown sugar
1 tablespoon cinnamon

Prepare the yeast.

In the bowl of a stand mixer with the hook attachment on, stir together the warm milk, granulated sugar, and yeast, then let it sit for about 5 minutes. Meanwhile, grease the muffin pans or line them with paper liners.

Combine the ingredients.

Add 2 tablespoons of room-temperature butter, 2½ cups of flour, the salt, and egg to the bowl. Mix on low with the hook attachment until well combined. Add more flour as needed, a little at a time, until a dough forms. Raise the speed to medium, and continue kneading for 4 to 6 minutes, or until dough is smooth and elastic.

Let the dough rise.

Grease a large bowl with oil. Add the dough, turn to coat, cover with plastic wrap and place in a warm, dark, draft-free place to double in size, about 1 hour.

Make the topping.

Meanwhile, place the melted butter in a small bowl. In another small bowl, mix together the brown sugar and cinnamon.

Form the dough.

Punch down the dough and divide it evenly into 18 pieces. Divide each piece into 4, and roll each into a ball in the palms of your hands. Dip the dough balls in the melted butter, then roll in the cinnamon sugar. Place 4 balls in each muffin cup, repeating until all dough is dipped and rolled. Discard any leftover butter or sugar. Lightly cover the dough, and place in a warm, dark, draft-free place for another hour or until risen again.

Preheat the oven to 350°F.

Bake for 15 to 20 minutes, or until golden brown. Cool slightly before removing from pan.

TRY INSTEAD: Instead of cinnamon, you can use another spice combination such as nutmeg or allspice.

HELPFUL HINT: These treats can be a little sticky, so I recommend using a nonstick pan or paper liners.

DID YOU KNOW? If you don't have a stand mixer, you can make the dough by hand with a large spoon.

soft pretzel sticks
WITH HONEY MUSTARD DIP

PREP TIME: 30 minutes (plus 1 hour for dough to rise)
COOK TIME: 17 minutes
YIELD: 24 pretzels

TOOLS/EQUIPMENT

- Stand mixer or large bowl
- Large gowl
- 2 baking sheets
- Parchment paper (optional)
- Large saucepan
- Slotted spoon
- Pastry brush
- Wire rack
- Small bowl

FOR THE PRETZELS

1½ cups warm water (105 to 115°F)
1 tablespoon granulated sugar
1 (¼-ounce) envelope active dry yeast
4 to 4½ cups all-purpose flour, plus more to flour the work surface
2 teaspoons table salt
4 tablespoons unsalted butter, melted
1 tablespoon vegetable or canola oil
Butter, for greasing the baking sheets (optional)

Prepare the yeast.
In the bowl of a stand mixer with the hook attachment on, stir together 1½ cups of warm water, sugar, and yeast until blended, then let it sit for about 5 minutes.

Blend the ingredients.
Add about 3½ cups of flour, the salt, and melted butter to the bowl. Mix on low with the hook attachment until well blended. Add more flour as needed for the dough to come together. Raise the speed to medium, and continue kneading for 4 to 6 minutes or until dough is smooth and elastic.

Let the dough rise.
Grease a large bowl with the oil, add the dough, turn it to coat, cover with plastic wrap and place in a warm, draft-free place to double in size, about 1 hour.

Preheat the oven to 450°F.
Generously grease 2 baking sheets or line with parchment paper.

Prepare the water bath.
In a large saucepan over high heat, add the 8 cups of water and baking soda. Bring to a boil, and stir to blend.

Form the pretzel sticks.
While waiting for the water to boil, place the risen dough on a lightly floured surface. Divide the dough in half, then divide each half into 12 balls, for a total of 24 balls. Roll out each ball into a rope 4 to 5 inches long. Dust off any excess flour from the pretzels. »

**FOR THE WATER BATH
AND TOPPING**

8 cups water

½ cup baking soda

1 egg yolk

1 to 2 teaspoons pretzel salt or
    coarse salt

FOR THE HONEY MUSTARD DIP

½ cup mayonnaise

¼ cup honey

¼ cup yellow mustard

Put the pretzels in the water bath.
Gently lower each pretzel into the boiling water,
2 or 3 at a time, and cook for 20 to 30 seconds.
Remove the pretzels with a large slotted spoon or
spatula, gently shaking off any excess water, then
place the pretzels on the baking sheets. Mix the
egg yolk with a little water to thin in a small bowl.
With a pastry brush, lightly brush the egg yolk on
top of the pretzels, then sprinkle with the pretzel
or coarse salt.

Bake the pretzels.
Bake for 12 to 17 minutes, or until dark golden
brown. Cool slightly, then transfer the pretzels to
a wire rack to finish cooling before serving.

Make the honey mustard dip.
In a small bowl, mix together the mayonnaise,
honey, and mustard, and serve alongside the
pretzels.

TRY INSTEAD: Instead of honey mustard, serve the pretzels with your
favorite chip dip.

quick and easy drop biscuits

PREP TIME: 15 minutes

COOK TIME: 12 minutes

YIELD: 18 biscuits

TOOLS/EQUIPMENT
- Medium bowl
- Pastry cutter (or fork or two knives; see Cutting in Butter, page 42)
- 2 baking sheets
- Parchment paper (optional)

2 cups all-purpose flour

2 teaspoons baking powder

½ teaspoon table salt

½ cup (1 stick) cold unsalted butter, cut into small cubes

¾ cup cold milk (2 percent or whole)

Preheat the oven to 425°F.

Mix the dry ingredients.

In a medium bowl, mix together the flour, baking powder, and salt until blended.

Cut in the butter.

Using a pastry cutter or the back of a fork, cut the butter into the flour mixture until the mixture is even and crumbly.

Add the wet ingredients.

Mix the milk into the flour mixture, and stir until the dough is just combined (don't overmix) and a soft moist dough forms.

Bake the biscuits.

Using a spoon, drop the biscuit dough onto 2 nonstick baking sheets or baking sheets lined with parchment paper to make 18 biscuits. Bake for 9 to 12 minutes, or until browned on the bottom.

TRY INSTEAD: Make garlic cheddar biscuits by adding 1 cup shredded Cheddar cheese and ½ teaspoon garlic powder to the dough.

TROUBLESHOOTING TIP: The dough should be soft and moist. If your dough is a little crumbly or dry, add a little more milk.

fluffy buttermilk chive biscuits

PREP TIME: 20 minutes

COOK TIME: 17 minutes

YIELD: 16 biscuits

TOOLS/EQUIPMENT

- Cast-iron pan or skillet (about 10½-inch diameter)
- Large bowl
- Pastry cutter
- 2-inch round cookie or biscuit cutter
- Pastry brush

Butter, for greasing the pan

2¾ cups plus 2 tablespoons all-purpose flour

4½ teaspoons baking powder

1 teaspoon table salt

6 tablespoons cold, cubed unsalted butter

½ cup chopped fresh chives

1 to 1½ cups cold buttermilk

Flour, for the work surface

3 tablespoons melted unsalted butter

Preheat the oven to 425°F.
Set the oven rack at the lowest level. Grease a cast-iron pan.

Mix the dry ingredients.
In a large bowl, mix together the flour, baking powder, and salt until combined.

Cut in the butter.
With a pastry cutter or back of a fork, cut in the 6 tablespoons of cold butter, until the mixture resembles coarse crumbs. Stir in the chives.

Add the wet ingredients.
Add 1 cup buttermilk to the flour mixture. Stir to combine, and add more milk as necessary until the dough just comes together but is still moist. Be careful not to overwork the dough or the biscuits may come out dry.

Form the biscuits.
Place the dough on a floured surface. Gently press the dough until 1 inch thick. With a 2-inch round cutter, cut the dough into 16 biscuits.

Bake the biscuits.
Place the biscuits next to each other in the prepared pan. Bake on the bottom rack for 12 to 17 minutes or until golden brown. Brush with the 3 tablespoons of melted butter. Cool slightly before serving.

TRY INSTEAD: Instead of chives, you can use chopped cooked bacon, shredded cheese, or even chopped precooked onion.

homemade mini cheese bagels

PREP TIME: 45 minutes (plus
1½ hours for dough to rise)

COOK TIME: 25 minutes

YIELD: 12 mini bagels

TOOLS/EQUIPMENT

- Stand mixer (optional)
  or large bowl
- Large bowl
- 2 baking sheets
- Large saucepan
- Slotted spoon

FOR THE BAGELS

1 cup warm water (105 to 115°F)
1 tablespoon granulated sugar
1 (¼-ounce) envelope active
    dry yeast
2½ to 3 cups all-purpose flour
1 teaspoon table salt
1 teaspoon olive oil, plus 1 to
    2 tablespoons olive oil, divided

FOR THE WATER BATH

8 cups water
1 tablespoon granulated sugar

FOR THE TOPPING

½ cup shredded Parmesan or
    Asiago cheese

Prepare the yeast.
In the bowl of a stand mixer with the hook
attachment on, stir together the 1 cup of water,
1 tablespoon of sugar, and the yeast, then let it
sit for about 5 minutes.

Make the dough.
Add 2 cups of flour and the salt to the bowl. Mix
on low with the hook attachment until well combined, adding more flour, a little at a time, until a
dough forms. Increase the speed to medium, and
continue kneading for 4 to 6 minutes or until the
dough is smooth and elastic.

Let it rise.
Grease a large bowl with oil. Add the dough, turn
it to coat, then cover with plastic wrap and place
in a warm, dark, draft-free place to double in size,
about 1 hour.

Prepare the baking sheet.
Generously grease the baking sheet with 1 or
2 tablespoons of olive oil, or line with parchment paper.

Form the bagels.
When the dough has doubled, punch it down.
Divide the dough into 12 balls. Roll each ball into
a log 5 to 6 inches long. Join the ends together,
place fingers through the hole and roll the ends
together until smooth. Place the bagels on the
prepared baking sheet. Cover the bagels with
a clean, light towel, and place in a warm, dark,
draft-free place for about 30 minutes or until
dough has risen a bit more.

Preheat the oven to 400°F.
Grease another baking sheet or line with parchment paper.

Prepare the water bath.
In a large saucepan over high heat, add the 8 cups of water and 1 tablespoon sugar. Bring to a boil, stirring to combine.

Dip the bagels in the water bath.
In batches, add a few bagels at a time to the boiling water for 20 seconds, then with a slotted spoon, turn the bagels over and cook an additional 20 seconds. Remove the bagels from the water, gently shaking off excess water, and place on the prepared baking sheet.

Bake the bagels.
Bake for 15 to 25 minutes or until golden brown. In the last 5 minutes of baking, sprinkle the bagels with the cheese and continue baking.

rosemary onion focaccia

PREP TIME: 30 minutes (plus 1 hour 20 minutes for dough to rise)

COOK TIME: 20 minutes

YIELD: 1 flat loaf (serves 12)

TOOLS/EQUIPMENT

- Stand mixer or large bowl
- Large bowl
- Plastic wrap
- Baking sheet
- Pastry brush

FOR THE BREAD

1 cup warm water (105 to 115°F)

2 tablespoons granulated sugar

1 (¼-ounce) envelope active dry yeast

3½ to 4 cups all-purpose flour

¼ cup plus 2 to 3 tablespoons olive oil, divided

1 teaspoon table salt

FOR THE TOPPING

2 tablespoons olive oil

½ small red onion, very thinly sliced

¼ cup shredded Parmesan cheese

2 garlic cloves, minced

½ teaspoon table salt

⅛ teaspoon freshly ground black pepper

2 tablespoons fresh rosemary

Prepare the yeast.

In the bowl of a stand mixer with the hook attachment on, stir together the warm water, sugar, and yeast, then let it sit for about 5 minutes.

Combine the ingredients.

Add 3 cups of flour, ¼ cup of olive oil, and 1 teaspoon of salt to the bowl. Mix on low with the hook attachment until well blended. Add more flour as needed, a little at a time, until a dough forms. Raise the speed to medium, and continue kneading for 4 to 6 minutes, or until the dough is smooth and elastic.

Let the dough rise.

Grease a large bowl with 1 tablespoon of olive oil. Add the dough, turn to coat, cover with plastic wrap and place in a warm, dark, draft-free place to double in size, about 1 hour.

Prepare the baking sheet.

Generously grease the baking sheet with 1 or 2 tablespoons of olive oil.

Form the bread.

Transfer the dough to the prepared baking sheet. Spread the dough out into a long oblong shape, about ½ inch thick. Cover loosely with plastic wrap and return to a warm, dark, draft-free place for 15 to 20 minutes to rest and rise slightly.

Preheat the oven to 400°F.

But first, place the oven rack at the lowest level.

Top the bread.

Remove the plastic wrap from the dough, and using your fingertips, gently push down on the dough to leave slight dimples. Brush 2 tablespoons of olive oil over the top of the dough. Lay the onion slices on top. Sprinkle the cheese, garlic, ½ teaspoon of salt, black pepper, and rosemary on top.

Bake the bread.

Bake on the lowest oven rack for 15 to 20 minutes, or until golden brown.

TRY INSTEAD: Instead of fresh rosemary, you can use other fresh herbs, such as chopped basil or oregano.

DID YOU KNOW? If you don't have a stand mixer, you can make the dough by hand with a large spoon.

TROUBLESHOOTING TIP: Check on your bread now and then. If the bread or the toppings appear to be getting too brown or burnt, simply cover the entire bread lightly with aluminum foil to protect it while it finishes baking.

old-fashioned white sandwich bread

PREP TIME: 30 minutes (plus 1½ hours for dough to rise)

COOK TIME: 40 minutes

YIELD: 2 loaves (serves 24)

TOOLS/EQUIPMENT

- Stand mixer or large bowl
- Large bowl
- Plastic wrap
- 2 loaf pans (8½ by 4½ by 2½ inches)
- Pastry brush
- Wire rack

FOR THE BREAD

2 cups warm milk (2 percent or whole, 105-115°F)

2 tablespoons granulated sugar

1 (¼-ounce) envelope active dry yeast

2 tablespoons butter, at room temperature

5 to 6 cups all-purpose flour

2 teaspoons table salt

1 tablespoon vegetable or canola oil

Butter, for greasing the pans

FOR THE TOPPING

2 tablespoons butter, melted

Prepare the yeast.

In the bowl of a stand mixer with the hook attachment on, stir together the warm milk, sugar, and yeast, then let it sit for about 5 minutes.

Combine the ingredients.

Add the 2 tablespoons room-temperature butter, 4 cups of flour, and salt to the yeast mixture. Mix on low with the hook attachment until well blended. Add more flour as needed, a little at a time, until a dough forms. Raise the speed to medium, and continue kneading for 4 to 6 minutes, or until the dough is smooth and elastic.

Let it rise.

Grease a large bowl with oil. Add the dough, turn it to coat, cover with plastic wrap and place in a warm, dark, draft-free place to double in size, about 1 hour. Punch down the dough, form it into 2 loaves, and place each in a greased loaf pan. Lightly brush the tops of the loaves with the melted butter. Cover with plastic wrap, and place in a warm, dark, draft-free place to rise again, about 30 minutes.

Preheat the oven to 350°F.

Bake the bread.

Bake for 30 to 40 minutes or until browned and hollow-sounding when lightly tapped. Cool slightly, then remove and place on a wire rack to finish cooling.

DID YOU KNOW? If you don't have a stand mixer, you can make the dough by hand with a large spoon.

HELPFUL HINT: To help the bread maintain its shape, cool bread completely before slicing with a serrated (jagged-edge) knife.

honey oat bread

PREP TIME: 20 minutes (plus 1 hour for dough to rise)
COOK TIME: 55 minutes
YIELD: 2 loaves (serves 24)

TOOLS/EQUIPMENT

- Large bowl
- Small saucepan
- Whisk or spoon
- 2 loaf pans (approximately 8½ by 4½ by 2½ inches)
- Aluminum foil
- Pastry brush
- Wire rack

1 (¼-ounce) envelope active dry yeast
¼ cup warm water (105 to 115°F)
2 cups milk (2 percent or whole)
4 tablespoons unsalted butter, divided
2 tablespoons honey
1 teaspoon table salt
1¼ cups old-fashioned rolled oats
4 to 5 cups all-purpose flour, plus more to flour the work surface
Butter, for greasing the pans

Prepare the yeast.
In a large bowl, stir together the yeast and warm water. Let sit for about 5 minutes.

Heat the milk.
In a small saucepan over medium heat, add the milk, 3 tablespoons of butter, the honey, and salt. Whisk until the butter has melted and the mixture is blended. Let this mixture cool a bit, then pour into the yeast mixture.

Blend the ingredients.
Add the oats and 4 cups of flour to the yeast mixture, and stir until well blended. Add more flour as needed until a sticky dough forms.

Knead the dough.
Place the dough on a well-floured surface. Knead the dough 6 to 8 minutes, adding flour as necessary, until smooth and elastic.

Let it rise.
Divide the dough in half, form into two loaves, and place each in a well-greased loaf pan. Cover lightly with plastic wrap and place in a dark, warm, draft-free place to double in size, about 1 hour.

Preheat the oven to 350°F.

Bake the bread.
Bake the bread for about 25 minutes, then cover with aluminum foil to prevent further browning. Continue baking for an additional 20 to 30 minutes or until the loaves sound hollow when lightly tapped. Melt the remaining tablespoon of butter and brush it on the tops of the loaves. Cool slightly, then transfer to a wire rack to finish cooling.

yogurt banana bread

PREP TIME: 20 minutes
COOK TIME: 60 minutes
YIELD: 1 loaf (serves 12)

TOOLS/EQUIPMENT
- Loaf pan (8½ by 4½ by 2½ inches)
- 2 medium bowls

Butter, for greasing the pan
Flour, for dusting the pan
1⅔ cups all-purpose flour
1 teaspoon baking soda
½ teaspoon cinnamon
½ teaspoon table salt
2 large eggs, at room temperature
¾ cup granulated sugar
1½ cups mashed, very ripe
  bananas (3 to 5 bananas)
½ cup vegetable or canola oil
2 tablespoons plain Greek yogurt
1 teaspoon vanilla extract

Preheat the oven to 350°F.
Lightly grease and flour a loaf pan.

Mix the dry ingredients.
In a medium bowl, mix together the flour, baking soda, cinnamon, and salt until well combined.

Mix remaining ingredients.
In another medium bowl, beat together the eggs and sugar for 3 to 5 minutes, or until light and fluffy. Stir in the banana, oil, yogurt, and vanilla until just combined.

Combine the ingredients.
Make a well in the center of the dry ingredients. Pour the wet ingredients into the well. Stir until just combined.

Bake the bread.
Pour the batter into the prepared loaf pan. Bake at 350°F for 45 to 60 minutes, or until a toothpick inserted in the center comes out clean.

TRY INSTEAD: For a different flavor, try adding ⅔ cup chopped nuts or mini chocolate chips to the batter.

TROUBLESHOOTING TIP: Make sure the inside of your oven is clean before baking. Leftover food that has fallen to the bottom of the oven can catch on fire, but it can also smoke, which can give your baked goods a smoky and funny smell and flavor!

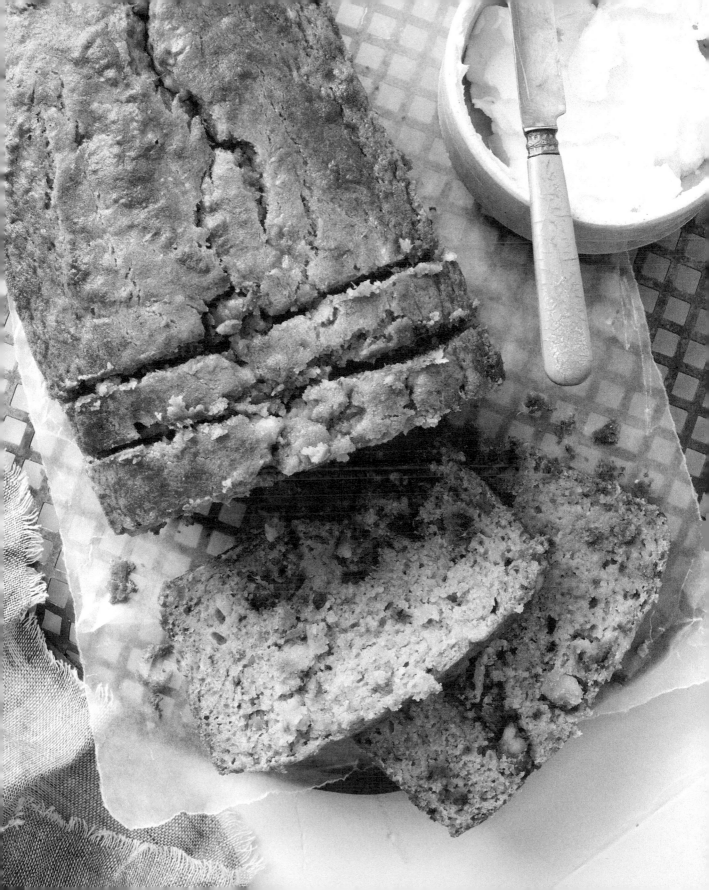

cakes & cupcakes

sprinkle cake pops

PREP TIME: 60 minutes
(plus 1 hour chill time)
COOK TIME: 25 minutes
YIELD: 24 cake pops

TOOLS/EQUIPMENT

- 9-inch round cake pan
- Medium bowl
- Large bowl
- Electric stand or hand mixer
- Wire rack
- Baking sheet
- Wax or parchment paper
- Double boiler (or see Make Your Own Double Boiler, page 53)
- Spatula
- White lollipop sticks
- Cake pop stand, box, or foam (see Pro Tip, page 88)

FOR THE CAKE

Butter, for greasing the pan
Flour, for dusting the pan
1 cup all-purpose flour
1 teaspoon baking powder
¼ teaspoon baking soda
¼ teaspoon table salt
⅓ cup unsalted butter,
    at room temperature
⅔ cup granulated sugar
2 large eggs, at room temperature
1½ teaspoons vanilla extract
⅓ cup milk (2 percent or whole)

Preheat the oven to 350°F.
Grease and lightly flour a 9-inch round cake pan.

Mix the dry ingredients.
In a medium bowl, stir together the flour, baking powder, baking soda, and salt.

Cream the butter and sugar.
In a large bowl, beat ⅓ cup of room-temperature butter with an electric mixer on medium speed for about 10 seconds or until smooth. Beat in the granulated sugar until well combined and light and fluffy, about 2 minutes. Beat in the eggs, one at a time, beating after each egg is added. Beat in the vanilla.

Combine the ingredients.
Alternate adding some of the flour mixture and ⅓ cup of milk to the butter mixture, beating on low after each addition, until the batter is just combined.

Bake the cake.
Pour the cake batter into the prepared pan. Bake for 20 to 25 minutes, or until a toothpick inserted into the middle comes out clean. Cool slightly, then remove the cake from the pan to finish cooling on a wire rack.

FOR THE FROSTING

4 tablespoons unsalted butter,
    at room temperature
2 cups confectioners' sugar
2 to 4 tablespoons milk (2 percent
    or whole)

FOR THE CANDY COATING

White candy melts, about
    2 (10-ounce) bags
Sprinkles

Make the frosting.

When the cake is completely cooled, prepare the frosting. In a medium bowl, add 4 tablespoons of room-temperature butter and beat with an electric mixer for about 10 seconds, or until smooth. Gradually beat in the confectioners' sugar. Add 2 tablespoons of milk and beat until smooth, adding a little more milk at a time as needed. The frosting should be a little on the thicker side.

Stir together the cake and frosting.

In a large bowl, crumble the cooled cake into pieces. Add ¼ cup of frosting. Using a sturdy spatula or large spoon, mix together the cake and frosting. Add a little more frosting at a time until the cake is fully crumbled and the mixture starts to clump together.

Form the cake balls.

Scoop the cake mixture out into 1-inch balls, roll in your hands if necessary to form a ball, and place on a baking sheet lined with wax or parchment paper. Refrigerate for about 1 hour, or until the cake balls are firm. »

TRY INSTEAD: Instead of sprinkles, substitute your favorite chopped candy, mini chocolate chips, or chopped nuts!

HELPFUL HINT: Make sure the cake is completely cooled before mixing with the frosting, otherwise, the frosting will melt and the cake will not mold into balls.

PRO TIP: You can buy a cake pop stand, which makes it easier to stand pops straight up after dipping. A stand also makes a festive display for serving. You can also poke holes in a box or use a block of foam to hold cake pops up.

Dip the cake balls.

Place the candy melts in the top of a double boiler. Place over boiling water, then reduce the heat to low. Stir constantly, until the candy melts are melted and smooth. Dip about ¼ inch of the tip of a lollipop stick into the melted candy melt, then insert the stick into the cake ball. Dip the cake balls, one at a time, in the candy melts, covering the entire cake ball and just below to the stick. You can pour the melted candy melts into a tall narrow container or glass for easier dipping. Before the candy melt hardens, sprinkle the sprinkles on top of the cake balls. Place the cake pops on a cake pop stand or in foam (see Pro Tip) to stand upright. Repeat with the remaining cake balls.

angel food cake

PREP TIME: 50 minutes

COOK TIME: 45 minutes

YIELD: 1 cake (serves 12)

TOOLS/EQUIPMENT

- Medium bowl
- Large bowl
- Stand mixer with whisk attachment or electric hand mixer
- Sifter (or mesh strainer)
- 10-inch tube pan (with removable bottom)
- Wire rack or sturdy glass bottle

1½ cups confectioners' sugar, sifted

1 cup all-purpose flour, sifted

1½ cups egg whites (from 10 to 12 large eggs)

1½ teaspoons cream of tartar

1 teaspoon vanilla extract

1 cup granulated sugar

Preheat the oven to 350°F.

But first, make sure the oven rack is in the lowest position.

Combine the sugar and flour.

In a medium bowl, mix together the confectioners' sugar and flour until well blended with no lumps.

Whip up the egg whites.

In a large bowl, add the egg whites (see Separating Eggs, page 29), cream of tartar, and vanilla. Beat on medium until the whites start getting foamy, 1 to 2 minutes. Increase the speed to medium-high, and continue beating until the egg whites become thick and opaque, 1 to 2 minutes.

Add the granulated sugar.

With the mixer on medium-high speed, slowly add the granulated sugar, 1 to 2 tablespoons at a time. Continue beating until the egg whites are shiny and stiff peaks form, 4 to 6 minutes.

TRY INSTEAD: Instead of vanilla extract, try another extract, such as lemon, coconut, or almond.

HELPFUL HINT: When baking angel food cake in a tube pan, the pan is never greased, because the batter clings to the sides of the pan, which helps it rise.

TROUBLESHOOTING TIP: Sifting your dry ingredients will prevent heavy lumps in this delicate cake. Also, bring your egg whites to room temperature for the best volume when beating. You can quickly warm cold eggs by covering the eggs in a bowl of warm tap water for 5 to 10 minutes.

Fold in the dry ingredients.

Gently sift about a quarter of the flour and confectioners' sugar mixture over the egg whites. Very gently fold in the flour mixture with a large rubber spatula, being careful to not deflate the egg whites. Repeat with the remaining flour and confectioners' sugar until just folded in.

Bake the cake.

Pour the batter into an ungreased 10-inch tube pan. Lightly run a butter knife through the batter to remove any air bubbles. Bake for 35 to 45 minutes, or until the top is lightly browned and springs back when lightly touched. Set the cake upside down over a wire rack or sturdy glass bottle to cool. When cooled, run a butter knife around the edge to loosen before inverting onto a plate.

lemon loaf cake

PREP TIME: 20 minutes

COOK TIME: 60 minutes

YIELD: 1 cake (serves 12)

TOOLS/EQUIPMENT

- Loaf pan (approximately 8½ by 4½ by 2½ inches)
- Small bowl
- Medium bowl
- Large bowl
- Electric hand mixer or stand mixer
- Zester
- Wire rack
- Whisk (or fork)

FOR THE CAKE

Butter, for greasing the pan

Flour, for dusting the pan

⅓ cup milk (2 percent or whole)

2 tablespoons freshly squeezed lemon juice

1½ cups all-purpose flour

¼ teaspoon baking powder

¼ teaspoon baking soda

¼ teaspoon table salt

½ cup (1 stick) unsalted butter, at room temperature

1 cup granulated sugar

2 large eggs, at room temperature

½ teaspoon vanilla extract

1 tablespoon freshly grated lemon zest

Preheat the oven to 350°F.

Grease and lightly flour a loaf pan.

Make the sour milk.

In a small bowl, add ⅓ cup of milk and 2 tablespoons of lemon juice, and stir to combine. Let sit about 10 minutes.

Mix the dry ingredients.

In a medium bowl, stir together the flour, baking powder, baking soda, and salt.

Cream the butter and sugar.

In a large bowl, beat the butter with an electric mixer on medium speed for about 10 seconds, or until smooth. Beat in the granulated sugar until well blended and light and fluffy, about 2 minutes. Beat in the eggs, one at a time, beating after each egg is added. Beat in the vanilla and lemon zest.

Combine all ingredients.

Alternate adding the flour mixture and the milk mixture to the butter mixture, beating on low after each addition, until the batter is just combined.

Bake the cake.

Pour the cake batter into the prepared pan. Bake for 45 to 60 minutes, or until a toothpick inserted into the middle comes out clean. Cool slightly, then remove the cake from the pan to finish cooling on a wire rack.

FOR THE GLAZE

¾ cup confectioners' sugar

2 teaspoons freshly squeezed
   lemon juice

1 to 3 tablespoons milk (2 percent
   or whole)

Make the glaze.

In a medium bowl, whisk together the confectioners' sugar, 2 teaspoons of lemon juice, and 1 tablespoon of milk. Whisk in more milk as needed until thick but spreadable. Spoon the glaze over the top of the cake, so it can drizzle down the sides.

TROUBLESHOOTING TIP: If you aren't getting much juice from your citrus fruit, use the palm of your hand to firmly roll the fruit on the counter, or microwave the fruit for 10 to 20 seconds before juicing.

TRY INSTEAD: For a stronger lemon flavor, use 1 teaspoon lemon extract instead of the vanilla extract.

HELPFUL HINT: Resist the urge to open the oven door while the cake is baking. The temperature of the oven will change quickly. Instead, use the oven light to check on things.

orange vanilla pound cake

PREP TIME: 30 minutes

COOK TIME: 90 minutes

YIELD: 1 cake (serves 16)

TOOLS/EQUIPMENT

- 1 (10-inch) tube pan
- Large bowl
- Electric hand mixer or stand mixer
- Zester
- Small saucepan
- Pastry brush

FOR THE CAKE

Butter, for greasing the pan

Flour, for dusting the pan

3 cups all-purpose flour

½ teaspoon baking powder

½ teaspoon table salt

1½ cups (3 sticks) unsalted butter, at room temperature

3 cups granulated sugar

5 large eggs, at room temperature

2 tablespoons freshly grated orange zest

2 teaspoons vanilla extract

1 cup milk (2 percent or whole)

FOR THE ORANGE GLAZE

½ cup granulated sugar

½ cup freshly squeezed orange juice (from 2 or 3 oranges)

Preheat the oven to 350°F.

Grease and flour a 10-inch tube pan.

Combine the dry ingredients.

In a large bowl, combine the flour, baking powder, and salt until well combined.

Cream the butter and sugar.

In a separate large bowl, beat the butter with an electric mixer on medium speed until smooth, about 10 seconds. Beat in 3 cups of sugar until well blended and light and fluffy, about 2 minutes. Beat in the eggs, one at a time, then beat in the orange zest and vanilla until blended.

Combine the ingredients.

Alternate beating in the dry ingredients and the milk into the butter mixture until just combined.

Bake the cake.

Pour the batter into the tube pan. Bake for 60 to 90 minutes, or until a toothpick inserted into the middle comes out clean.

Prepare the glaze.

In a small saucepan over medium heat, heat ½ cup of sugar and orange juice, stirring until slightly thickened, about 5 minutes. Brush the glaze over the top and sides of the warm cake.

 HELPFUL HINT: For best results, don't substitute margarine for butter in this recipe.

cinnamon nut coffee cake

PREP TIME: 30 minutes
COOK TIME: 60 minutes
YIELD: 1 cake (serves 16)

TOOLS/EQUIPMENT

- 10-inch tube pan
  (with removable bottom)
- Small bowl
- 2 large bowls
- Electric hand mixer
  or stand mixer
- Wire rack

Butter, for greasing the pan
Flour, for dusting the pan

FOR THE FILLING

½ cup granulated sugar
1 cup chopped walnuts or pecans
1½ teaspoons cinnamon

FOR THE CAKE

2¼ cups all-purpose flour
2 teaspoons baking powder
½ teaspoon baking soda
¼ teaspoon table salt
⅓ cup unsalted butter, at room
    temperature
1 cup granulated sugar
⅓ cup vegetable or canola oil
2 large eggs, at room temperature
2 teaspoons vanilla extract
1 cup sour cream or plain Greek
    yogurt

Preheat the oven to 350°F.
Grease and flour a 10-inch tube pan.

Make the filling.
In a small bowl, mix together ½ cup of sugar, the walnuts or pecans, and cinnamon until well combined.

Blend the dry ingredients.
In a large bowl, mix the flour, baking powder, baking soda, and salt until well blended.

Cream the butter and sugar.
In a separate large bowl, beat the butter with an electric mixer on medium speed for about 10 seconds, or until smooth. Beat in 1 cup of sugar and the oil, until well blended and light and fluffy, about 2 minutes. Beat in the eggs, one at a time, beating after each egg is added. Beat in the vanilla, then beat in the sour cream.

Combine the ingredients.
Slowly beat the butter mixture into the dry ingredients until just blended.

Assemble the cake.
Spoon half of the cake batter into the tube pan. Spread with a spoon to form an even layer across the bottom of the pan. Sprinkle half of the nut filling over the batter, then top with the remaining batter.

Bake the cake.
Bake for 45 to 60 minutes, or until a toothpick inserted into the middle comes out clean. Cool slightly, then remove from the pan to cool completely on a wire rack.

pick-your-flavor ice cream cake

PREP TIME: 30 minutes (plus
1 to 2 hours freezing time)
COOK TIME: 25 minutes
YIELD: 1 cake (serves 16)

TOOLS/EQUIPMENT

- 2 (9-inch) cake pans
- Medium bowl
- Large bowl
- Wire rack
- Small saucepan

FOR THE CAKE

Butter, for greasing the pans
Flour, for dusting the pans
1½ cups all-purpose flour
½ cup unsweetened cocoa powder
1 teaspoon baking powder
¼ teaspoon baking soda
¾ cup granulated sugar
½ cup brown sugar
¾ cup (1½ sticks) unsalted butter,
    melted and cooled
2 large eggs, at room temperature
1 teaspoon vanilla extract
1 cup milk (2 percent or whole)
4 cups ice cream, any flavor

FOR THE CHOCOLATE TOPPING

1 cup semisweet chocolate chips
2 teaspoons corn syrup
½ cup heavy whipping cream

Preheat the oven to 350°F.
Grease and lightly flour 2 (9-inch) round
cake pans.

Blend the flour mixture.
In a medium bowl, mix together the flour, cocoa
powder, baking powder, and baking soda until
well blended.

Blend the sugar and butter.
In a large bowl, mix the granulated sugar, brown
sugar, and butter until well blended, about
2 minutes. Add the eggs one at time, beating
after each addition, then beat in the vanilla.

Combine the ingredients.
Alternate beating in the dry ingredients and the
milk to the wet ingredients until just combined.

Bake the cakes.
Pour the batter evenly into the 2 prepared pans.
Bake for 20 to 25 minutes, or until a toothpick
inserted into the middle comes out clean. Cool
slightly, then remove from pans and place on a
wire rack to cool completely.

Assemble the cake.
Let the ice cream sit on the counter for 5 to
10 minutes, until soft but not soupy. Place the
bottom cake layer, flat side up, on a serving plate.
Spoon the ice cream on top of the bottom cake
layer, and spread the ice cream to the edge of the
cake with a spoon. Top with the other cake layer,
flat side down, and press gently on the cake to
help spread the ice cream to the edges. Place the
cake in the freezer for 1 to 2 hours, or until firm.

Prepare the topping.

In a medium bowl, add the chocolate chips and corn syrup. In a small saucepan over low heat, heat the heavy cream, whisking continuously, until it just starts to boil. Pour the hot cream over the chocolate chips. Let sit about 1 minute, then stir to combine until smooth. Let cool.

Top the cake.

Spoon the cooled chocolate over the top of the cake and let it drip down the sides of the cake. Return the cake to the freezer until ready to serve, at least a half hour. Let the cake sit at room temperature for 10 to 20 minutes to soften before slicing and serving.

zebra marble cake
WITH VANILLA FROSTING

PREP TIME: 30 minutes

COOK TIME: 45 minutes

YIELD: 1 cake (serves 8)

TOOLS/EQUIPMENT

- 1 (9-inch) round cake pan
- Medium bowl
- Large bowl
- Electric hand mixer or stand mixer
- Whisk or fork
- Wire rack

FOR THE CAKE

Butter, for greasing the pan

Flour, for dusting the pan

2 cups all-purpose flour

2 teaspoons baking powder

¼ teaspoon table salt

1 cup granulated sugar

4 large eggs, at room temperature

1 cup vegetable or canola oil

1 cup milk (2 percent or whole)

1 teaspoon vanilla extract

3 tablespoons sifted unsweetened cocoa powder

FOR THE FROSTING

½ cup (1 stick) butter, at room temperature

1¾ cups confectioners' sugar

½ teaspoon vanilla extract

⅛ teaspoon table salt

3 to 5 tablespoons milk (2 percent or whole)

Preheat the oven to 350˚F.

Grease and flour a 9-inch round cake pan.

Mix the dry ingredients.

In a medium bowl, stir together the flour, baking powder, and ¼ teaspoon of salt.

Blend the sugar and eggs.

In a large bowl, beat together the granulated sugar and eggs with an electric mixer on medium until well blended, about 2 minutes. Add the oil, 1 cup of milk, and 1 teaspoon of vanilla, beating until well blended.

Combine the ingredients.

Add the flour mixture to the egg mixture, beating on medium until just blended.

Make the chocolate batter.

Spoon half of the batter into a separate bowl. Whisk the cocoa powder into one of the bowls, stirring to blend.

Assemble the cake.

To make stripes, alternate adding the two batters to the pan. Spoon about 3 tablespoons of vanilla batter into the center of the pan. Then spoon about 3 tablespoons of chocolate batter in the middle of the pan on top of the vanilla batter. Repeat until all the batter is in the pan. The cake batter will spread to the edge of the pan as you add more. »

TRY INSTEAD: Instead of chocolate and vanilla, try dyeing the 2 bowls of cake batter with your favorite colors using food coloring!

TROUBLESHOOTING TIP: If stripes don't appear when you cut into the cake, you may have shaken the pan too much while adding the cake batter, or perhaps you varied the amount of batter you added to the pan each time (too much or too little at once). The good news is, it will still taste great!

Bake the cake.

Bake for 30 to 45 minutes, or until a toothpick inserted into the middle comes out clean. Let the cake cool slightly in the pan, then remove from the pan and place on a wire rack to finish cooling.

Make the frosting.

In a medium bowl, beat together the butter and confectioners' sugar with an electric mixer on medium speed. Beat in ½ teaspoon of vanilla and ⅛ teaspoon of salt. Add a little milk if necessary to thin the frosting. Spread the frosting over the cooled cake.

mini almond flourless chocolate cakes

PREP TIME: 10 minutes
COOK TIME: 30 minutes
YIELD: 4 cakes

TOOLS/EQUIPMENT

- 4 (4-ounce) ramekins
- Baking sheet
- Double boiler (or see Make Your Own Double Boiler, page 53)
- Medium bowl
- Whisk or fork

Butter, for greasing the ramekins
6 tablespoons unsalted butter
¼ cup honey
⅔ cup dark chocolate chips
1 cup finely ground almonds (or almond flour)
2 large eggs, at room temperature, beaten
1 teaspoon vanilla extract
½ teaspoon table salt

Preheat the oven to 350°F.
Lightly grease 4 small ramekins and place them on a baking sheet.

Melt the chocolate.
Add the butter, honey, and chocolate chips to the top of a double boiler over boiling water, then reduce the heat to low, mixing until smooth. Set aside to cool completely, about 30 to 45 minutes.

Whisk the ingredients.
In a medium bowl, whisk together the almonds, eggs, vanilla, and salt until well blended. Slowly whisk in the cooled chocolate mixture.

Bake the cakes.
Bake for 20 to 30 minutes, or until a toothpick inserted into the middle comes out clean.

TRY INSTEAD: Instead of dark chocolate chips, substitute semisweet or bittersweet for a different flavor. You can also top this with fresh berries and whipped cream!

HELPFUL HINT: If you don't have 4-ounce ramekins, you can use 6- or 8-ounce ones, but they may cook more quickly, so you may need to adjust the baking time.

FOOD FACT: It takes approximately 400 cacao beans to make one pound of chocolate!

chocolate fudge layer cake
WITH PEANUT BUTTER FROSTING

PREP TIME: 30 minutes

COOK TIME: 35 minutes

YIELD: 1 (2-layer) cake (serves 16)

TOOLS/EQUIPMENT

- 2 (9-inch) round cake pans
- Medium bowl
- Large bowl
- Electric hand mixer or stand mixer
- Wire rack
- Offset spatula or butter knife

FOR THE CAKE

Butter, for greasing the pans

Flour, for dusting the pans

2 cups all-purpose flour

¾ cup unsweetened cocoa powder

1 teaspoon baking soda

¾ teaspoon baking powder

½ teaspoon table salt

¾ cup (1½ sticks) unsalted butter, at room temperature

2 cups granulated sugar

3 large eggs, at room temperature

2 teaspoons vanilla extract

1½ cups milk (2 percent or whole)

1 cup mini chocolate chips

FOR THE FROSTING

1 cup (2 sticks) unsalted butter, at room temperature

1¼ cups creamy peanut butter

3 cups confectioners' sugar

1 to 2 tablespoons milk (2 percent or whole)

Preheat the oven to 350°F.
Grease and lightly flour 2 (9-inch) round cake pans.

Mix the dry ingredients.
In a medium bowl, stir together the flour, cocoa powder, baking soda, baking powder, and salt.

Cream the butter and sugar.
In a large bowl, beat ¾ cup of butter with an electric mixer on medium speed for about 10 seconds, or until smooth. Beat in the granulated sugar until well blended and light and fluffy, about 2 minutes. Beat in the eggs, one at a time, beating after each egg is added. Beat in the vanilla.

Combine the ingredients.
Alternate adding the flour mixture and 1½ cups of milk to the butter mixture, beating on low after each addition until batter is just combined. Fold in the chocolate chips.

Bake the cake.
Spoon the batter evenly among the 2 prepared cake pans. Bake for 30 to 35 minutes, or until a toothpick inserted into the center comes out clean. Cool slightly, then remove the cakes from the pans to finish cooling on a wire rack.

TRY INSTEAD: Like mocha? Try dissolving a little instant coffee in the milk for the cake batter for a richer chocolate flavor in the cake.

DID YOU KNOW? You can decorate the outside of the cake any way you'd like—so get creative! Add some mini chocolate chips, crushed peanuts, crushed candy, or cookies on the sides or top of the cake.

TROUBLESHOOTING TIP: This recipe makes just enough frosting for a thin layer around the cake and between the layers. If you like a lot of frosting, double the frosting recipe. Or just put the frosting in between the layers and on top of the cake, leaving the sides cakey for a rustic, natural look!

Make the frosting.
In a large bowl, blend 1 cup of butter and the peanut butter with an electric mixer on low speed. Beat in the confectioners' sugar. Slowly add 1 to 2 tablespoons of milk, beating until the frosting is a spreading consistency.

Frost the cake.
When the cakes are completely cool, place one layer, flat side up, on a serving plate. Spread the frosting over the top with an offset spatula or butter knife. Place the second cake layer on top, flat side down. Spread more frosting on the top and sides of cake as desired.

grasshopper cake stacks

PREP TIME: 30 minutes

COOK TIME: 25 minutes

YIELD: 15 cakes

TOOLS/EQUIPMENT

- 2 (9-inch) round cake pans
- Medium bowl
- Large bowl
- Electric hand mixer or stand mixer
- Wire rack
- 2-inch round cookie or biscuit cutter

FOR THE CAKES

Butter, for greasing the pans

Flour, for dusting the pans

1⅓ cups all-purpose flour

½ cup unsweetened cocoa powder

¾ teaspoon baking soda

½ teaspoon baking powder

¼ teaspoon table salt

½ cup (1 stick) unsalted butter, at room temperature

1⅓ cups granulated sugar

2 large eggs, at room temperature

1 teaspoon vanilla extract

1 cup milk (2 percent or whole)

Preheat the oven to 350°F.

Grease and lightly flour 2 (9-inch) round cake pans.

Mix the dry ingredients.

In a medium bowl, stir together the flour, cocoa powder, baking soda, baking powder, and salt.

Cream the butter and sugar.

In a large bowl, beat ½ cup of butter with an electric mixer on medium speed for about 10 seconds, or until smooth. Beat in the granulated sugar until well blended and light and fluffy, about 2 minutes. Add the eggs, one at a time, beating after each egg is added. Beat in the vanilla.

Blend the ingredients.

In batches, alternate adding the flour mixture and 1 cup of milk to the butter mixture, beating on low after each addition until the batter is just combined.

Bake the cake.

Spoon the batter evenly between two prepared cake pans. Bake for 20 to 25 minutes, or until a toothpick inserted into the center comes out clean. Cool slightly, then remove the cakes from pans to finish cooling on a wire rack.

Make the cake rounds.

Using a 2-inch round cookie cutter, cut cake into small rounds. You should get about 15 per pan for a total of 30. Save the cake scraps for other uses (see Did You Know?).

FOR THE MINT CHOCOLATE CHIP FROSTING

¾ cup (1½ sticks) unsalted butter, at room temperature

1 (16-ounce) bag (3¾ cups) confectioners' sugar

2 to 4 tablespoons milk (2 percent or whole)

1 teaspoon mint extract

Green food coloring

1 cup finely chopped semisweet chocolate, plus more for garnish (optional)

Prepare the frosting.

Beat together ¾ cup of butter and the confectioners' sugar with an electric mixer on medium speed. Slowly add the milk, 1 tablespoon at a time, until it has a frosting consistency. Beat in the mint extract and a few drops of green food coloring until well blended. Add a little more green food coloring as needed to achieve the desired color. Stir in the chopped chocolate.

Assemble the cakes.

Spread about 1 tablespoon of frosting over each cake round. Then place one frosted cake round on another to make 15 cakes in total. Garnish with chopped chocolate, if desired.

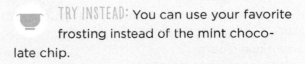 TRY INSTEAD: You can use your favorite frosting instead of the mint chocolate chip.

 DID YOU KNOW? Cake crumbs are great on top of ice cream!

HELPFUL HINT: To flour the pan, combine a little flour and unsweetened cocoa powder in a small bowl, mix, then dust over the pan. Flip the pan over a sink, and tap lightly to remove excess. Save a little of the mixture. Then, when cutting the cake rounds, dip your cookie cutter in a little flour to make cutting easier.

dark chocolate fudge lava cakes

PREP TIME: 20 minutes
COOK TIME: 12 minutes
YIELD: 4 cakes

TOOLS/EQUIPMENT

- 4 (6-ounce) ramekins
- Baking sheet
- Double boiler (or see Make Your Own Double Boiler, page 53)
- Medium bowl
- Electric hand mixer
- Spatula

Butter, for greasing the ramekins
Flour, for dusting the ramekins
½ cup (1 stick) unsalted butter
6 ounces dark chocolate, chopped
¼ cup granulated sugar
2 large eggs, at room temperature
2 large egg yolks
⅛ teaspoon table salt
2 tablespoons all-purpose flour

Preheat the oven to 350°F.
Grease and lightly flour 4 (6-ounce) ramekins. Set the ramekins on a baking sheet.

Melt the chocolate.
Place the butter and the chocolate in the top of a double boiler over boiling water, reduce the heat to low, and mix until smooth. Remove from heat, and cool completely.

Blend the ingredients.
In a medium bowl, beat the sugar, eggs, egg yolks, and salt with an electric mixer on medium speed until frothy. With a spatula, fold in the cooled chocolate, along with the flour, until just combined.

Bake the cakes.
Spoon the batter into the prepared ramekins. Bake for 10 to 12 minutes or until the sides of the cakes look firm but the center still looks a little soft. Cool the cakes for 1 to 2 minutes, then using oven mitts, gently flip them over onto serving plates. Let them sit a few seconds, then wiggle the ramekins slightly to allow the cakes to come out. If the cakes are stuck, gently loosen the edges with a butter knife. Serve immediately.

TRY INSTEAD: Instead of dark chocolate, you can use bittersweet or semisweet chocolate.

DID YOU KNOW? These cakes are great served with ice cream, whipped cream, and/or fresh berries!

upside-down apple cupcakes

PREP TIME: 30 minutes

COOK TIME: 20 minutes

YIELD: 18 cupcakes

TOOLS/EQUIPMENT

- 2 muffin pans
- Medium skillet
- Medium bowl
- Large bowl
- Electric mixer

Butter, for greasing the pans

FOR THE APPLES

4 tablespoons unsalted butter

⅔ cup brown sugar

2 large apples, cored, peeled, and very thinly sliced

FOR THE CAKES

1 cup all-purpose flour

1¼ teaspoons baking powder

½ teaspoon cinnamon

¼ teaspoon table salt

½ cup (1 stick) unsalted butter, at room temperature

1 cup granulated sugar

1 large egg

1 teaspoon vanilla extract

¼ cup buttermilk

Preheat the oven to 350°F.

Generously grease 18 cups of 2 (12-cup) muffin pans.

Cook the apples.

In a medium skillet over medium heat, heat 4 tablespoons of butter and the brown sugar, stirring until combined and melted. Add the apples, stirring to combine, and cook for 4 to 5 minutes or until the apples are soft, stirring occasionally. Spoon 2 or 3 apple slices and a little sauce into the bottom of each muffin cup.

Mix the dry ingredients.

In a medium bowl, stir together the flour, baking powder, cinnamon, and salt.

Cream the butter and sugar.

In a large bowl, beat ½ cup of room-temperature butter with an electric mixer on medium speed for about 10 seconds, or until smooth. Beat in the granulated sugar until well blended and light and fluffy, about 2 minutes. Add the eggs, one at a time, beating after each egg is added, then beat in the vanilla. »

TRY INSTEAD: Instead of apple, you could try pear, peach, or chopped pineapple.

DID YOU KNOW? These mini cakes are great served with vanilla ice cream or whipped cream!

HELPFUL HINT: When alternating flour and liquid in a cake recipe, generally it's best to add the dry and wet ingredients in two or three batches, starting with and ending with the dry ingredients. Adding too much wet mixture at once can cause the batter to separate, while adding too much dry mixture at once can lead to overmixing and a tougher cake.

Combine the ingredients.
In batches, alternate adding the flour mixture and the buttermilk to the butter mixture, beating on low after each addition until the batter is just combined.

Bake the cupcakes.
Spoon the batter over the apples in the muffin cups until half to ⅔ full. Bake for 18 to 20 minutes, or until a toothpick inserted into the center comes out clean. Cool slightly, then gently flip the cakes over onto a platter or serving plate.

coconut explosion cupcakes

PREP TIME: 30 minutes

COOK TIME: 20 minutes

YIELD: 12 cupcakes

TOOLS/EQUIPMENT

- Muffin pan
- Paper liners (optional)
- Medium bowl
- Large bowl
- Electric hand mixer or stand mixer
- Wire rack
- Spatula

FOR THE CUPCAKES

Butter, for greasing the pan (optional)

Flour, for dusting the pan (optional)

1 cup all-purpose flour

½ teaspoon baking powder

½ teaspoon baking soda

⅛ teaspoon table salt

¼ cup shortening, at room temperature

¾ cup granulated sugar

2 large egg whites

½ teaspoon vanilla extract

½ teaspoon coconut extract

¾ cup sweetened flaked coconut

⅔ cup buttermilk

FOR THE FROSTING

1 (8-ounce brick) cream cheese, at room temperature

6 tablespoons shortening, softened

½ teaspoon coconut extract

3 to 4 cups confectioners' sugar

½ cup sweetened flaked coconut

Milk (2 percent or whole, optional)

Preheat the oven to 350˚F.

Grease and lightly flour a 12-cup muffin pan or line with paper liners.

Mix the dry ingredients.

In a medium bowl, stir together the flour, baking powder, baking soda, and salt.

Cream the shortening and sugar.

In a large bowl, beat ¼ cup of shortening with an electric mixer on medium speed for about 10 seconds, or until smooth. Beat in the granulated sugar until well blended and light and fluffy, about 2 minutes. Beat in the egg whites, one at a time, beating after each is added. Beat in the vanilla and ½ teaspoon of coconut extract. Fold in ¾ cup of flaked coconut.

Combine the ingredients.

Alternate adding the flour mixture and the buttermilk to the shortening mixture, beating on low after each addition until batter is just blended.

Bake the cupcakes.

Spoon the batter into muffin cups about ⅔ full. Bake for 18 to 20 minutes, or until a toothpick inserted into the center comes out clean. Cool slightly, then remove the cupcakes to finish cooling on a wire rack. »

TRY INSTEAD: If you can't find coconut extract, you can substitute vanilla extract or even almond extract.

DID YOU KNOW? Using egg whites instead of whole eggs, and shortening instead of butter, gives these cupcakes a nice white color. If desired, you can substitute one whole egg for the two egg whites, and butter for the shortening.

HELPFUL HINT: Garnish the tops of cupcakes with toasted coconut if desired. To make toasted coconut, spread sweetened flaked coconut in a single layer on a baking sheet. Bake in a preheated 350°F oven for 5 to 10 minutes, stirring occasionally, until crispy and golden brown. Keep an eye on it because it can burn quickly!

Make the frosting.

In a large bowl, beat together the cream cheese and 6 tablespoons of shortening until smooth. Beat in ½ teaspoon of coconut extract. Beat in 2 cups of confectioners' sugar, adding more as needed while beating until a spreading consistency. Fold in ½ cup of flaked coconut. If the frosting is too thick, you can stir in a little milk, a few teaspoons at a time.

Frost the cupcakes.

When the cupcakes are completely cooled, frost the cupcakes with a spatula.

roasted strawberry shortcakes

PREP TIME: 25 minutes

COOK TIME: 25 minutes

YIELD: 6 shortcakes

TOOLS/EQUIPMENT

- Baking sheet
- Parchment paper (optional)
- Medium bowl
- Small bowl
- Whisk (or fork)
- Pastry cutter (see Cutting in Butter, page 42)
- Large spoon
- Pastry brush
- Wire rack
- Large bowl
- Electric hand mixer or stand mixer

FOR THE BISCUITS

Butter, for greasing the baking sheet (optional)

2 cups all-purpose flour

2 tablespoons granulated sugar

1 tablespoon baking powder

½ teaspoon table salt

⅓ cup plus 1 tablespoon cold heavy whipping cream, divided

⅓ cup water

1 large egg

4 tablespoons cold unsalted butter, cubed

Preheat the oven to 375°F.

Lightly grease a baking sheet or line with parchment paper.

Mix the dry ingredients.

In a medium bowl, mix together the flour, 2 tablespoons of sugar, baking powder, and salt.

Mix the wet ingredients.

In a small bowl, whisk together ⅓ cup of heavy cream, the water, and egg until well blended.

Cut in the butter.

Using a pastry cutter or the back of a fork, cut the butter into the flour mixture until the mixture is crumbly. Stir in the wet ingredients until just combined.

Bake the biscuits.

Using a large spoon, drop the biscuit dough onto the prepared baking sheet to make 6 biscuits, leaving about 2 inches of space in between. Brush 1 tablespoon of heavy cream over the top of the biscuits. Bake for 20 to 25 minutes, or until golden brown. Cool slightly, then transfer the biscuits to a wire rack to finish cooling. Keep the oven on for the strawberries.

FOR THE STRAWBERRIES
1½ pounds fresh strawberries, tops removed and thinly sliced
¼ cup granulated sugar
½ teaspoon vanilla extract

FOR THE WHIPPED CREAM
1½ cups cold heavy whipping cream
2 tablespoons granulated sugar

TRY INSTEAD: Instead of making your own whipped cream, you can use store-bought whipped cream or whipped topping.

DID YOU KNOW? If you don't want to get out an electric mixer, you can make whipped cream with a whisk. Simply whip the whipped cream until soft peaks form. Be forewarned, it takes a while and your arm may get tired!

Make the strawberries.
Lightly grease another baking sheet or line with parchment paper. Place the strawberry slices on the pan and toss gently with ¼ cup of sugar. Bake for 10 to 15 minutes, or until soft. Spoon the berries into a small bowl, and stir in the vanilla. Set aside to cool.

Make the whipped cream.
In a large, cold bowl, add 1½ cups of heavy cream and 2 tablespoons of sugar. Whip with an electric mixer on medium-high until soft peaks form.

Assemble the shortcakes.
Cut the biscuits in half to make a top and a bottom. Place the bottom half on serving plates, then spoon the strawberries and whipped cream on top. Cover with the top half of the biscuit. Serve immediately.

5

cookies & bars

snickerdoodle bites

PREP TIME: 20 minutes
(plus 1 hour chill time)
COOK TIME: 12 minutes
YIELD: 30 cookies

TOOLS/EQUIPMENT

- Small bowl
- Large bowl
- Electric hand mixer
- Plastic wrap
- 2 baking sheets
- Parchment paper (optional)
- Wire rack

FOR THE COOKIES

1¼ cups plus 2 tablespoons
   all-purpose flour
1 teaspoon cream of tartar
½ teaspoon baking soda
⅛ teaspoon table salt
½ cup (1 stick) unsalted butter,
   at room temperature
¾ cup granulated sugar
1 large egg
½ teaspoon vanilla extract

FOR THE TOPPING

3 tablespoons granulated sugar
1 teaspoon cinnamon

Mix the dry ingredients.
In a small bowl, stir together the flour, cream of tartar, baking soda, and salt.

Cream the butter and sugar.
In a large bowl, beat the butter with an electric mixer on medium speed for about 10 seconds, or until smooth. Beat in ¾ cup of sugar until well blended and light and fluffy, about 2 minutes. Beat in the egg, then beat in the vanilla until well blended.

Beat the ingredients.
Add the flour mixture to the butter and sugar mixture, beating with an electric mixer on medium speed until blended.

Refrigerate the dough.
Cover the bowl with plastic wrap and refrigerate to chill for about an hour, or until dough is firm and cold.

Preheat the oven to 350˚F.

Prepare the topping.
In a small bowl, mix together 3 tablespoons of sugar and the cinnamon in a small bowl until well blended.

Make the cookies.

Form the dough into 30 balls, about 2 teaspoons each. Roll each ball lightly in the cinnamon sugar mixture. Place the dough on 2 ungreased baking sheets, or baking sheets lined with parchment paper, leaving about 2 inches between cookies.

Bake the cookies.

Bake for 7 to 12 minutes or until lightly browned around the edges, rotating the pans halfway through cooking. Cool slightly, then transfer the cookies to a wire rack to cool completely.

TRY INSTEAD: Instead of cinnamon, you can experiment with other spices. Try nutmeg or allspice, or skip the spices and sugar and dip into rainbow sprinkles!

HELPFUL HINT: Chilled dough will really help make for easy shaping into balls. A small ice cream trigger scoop works great for balling the dough.

shortbread dippin' sticks

PREP TIME: 20 minutes (plus 30 minutes chill time)
COOK TIME: 20 minutes
YIELD: 36 cookies

TOOLS/EQUIPMENT

- Small bowl
- Large bowl
- Electric hand mixer
- Plastic wrap
- Rolling pin
- Cookie cutter (optional)
- 2 baking sheets
- Parchment paper (optional)
- Wire rack

3½ cups all-purpose flour
¼ teaspoon table salt
1½ cups (3 sticks) unsalted butter, at room temperature
1 cup granulated sugar
1 teaspoon vanilla extract
Flour, for dusting the work surface
Ice cream toppings like chocolate sauce, caramel, and strawberry sauce for dipping (optional)

Preheat the oven to 350°F.

Mix the dry ingredients.
In a small bowl, stir together the flour and salt.

Cream the butter and sugar.
In a large bowl, beat the butter with an electric mixer on medium speed for about 10 seconds, or until smooth. Beat in the sugar until light and fluffy, about 2 minutes. Beat in the vanilla.

Beat the ingredients.
Add the flour mixture to the butter and sugar mixture, and beat with an electric mixer on medium speed until blended.

Refrigerate the dough.
Wrap dough completely in plastic wrap. Flatten to form a large, flat disk. Refrigerate dough for 30 minutes to one hour, or until cold and firm.

Cut out the cookies.
Unwrap the dough and place on a lightly floured surface. Roll out dough to about a ½-inch thickness. Using a knife or cookie cutter, cut the dough into rectangles, about 1 inch by 2 inches.

Bake the cookies.
Place the cookies on 2 ungreased baking sheets or baking sheets lined with parchment paper, leaving about 2 inches between cookies. Bake for 15 to 20 minutes, or until lightly browned around the edges, rotating the pans halfway through cooking. Cool slightly, then transfer the cookies to a wire rack to cool completely. Serve with sauces for dipping.

spiced oatmeal raisin cookies

PREP TIME: 20 minutes
(plus 2 hours chill time)
COOK TIME: 17 minutes
YIELD: 12 cookies

TOOLS/EQUIPMENT

- Medium bowl
- Large bowl
- Electric mixer
- Plastic wrap
- Baking sheets
- Parchment paper (optional)
- Wire rack

1¼ cups old-fashioned rolled oats

¾ cup all-purpose flour

¾ teaspoon cinnamon

½ teaspoon table salt

½ teaspoon baking powder

⅛ teaspoon ground cloves

⅛ teaspoon ground nutmeg

⅛ teaspoon ground ginger

½ cup (1 stick) unsalted butter,
    at room temperature

¾ cup granulated sugar

2 tablespoons molasses

1 large egg

1 teaspoon vanilla extract

1 cup raisins

Mix the dry ingredients.

In a medium bowl, stir together the oats, flour, cinnamon, salt, baking powder, cloves, nutmeg, and ginger.

Cream the butter and sugar.

In a large bowl, beat the butter with an electric mixer on medium speed for about 10 seconds or until smooth. Beat in the sugar and molasses until well blended and light and fluffy, about 2 minutes. Beat in the egg, then beat in vanilla until well blended.

Beat the ingredients.

Add the flour mixture to the butter and sugar mixture, and beat with an electric mixer on medium speed until blended. With a spoon, stir in the raisins.

Refrigerate the dough.

Cover the dough with plastic wrap and refrigerate for at least 2 hours or overnight to firm up.

Preheat the oven to 350°F. ››

TRY INSTEAD: Instead of raisins, you can substitute another chewy dried fruit, like chopped dried cherries.

HELPFUL HINT: You don't have to refrigerate the dough, but doing so does seem to improve the taste and texture of the cookies!

FOOD FACT: Half of the world's raisin supply is grown in California!

Bake the cookies.

Drop the cookie dough in big (3-tablespoon) lumps onto ungreased baking sheets or baking sheets lined with parchment paper, leaving about 2 inches between cookies. Bake for 13 to 17 minutes, or until golden brown around the edges, rotating the pans halfway through cooking. Cool slightly, then transfer the cookies to a wire rack to cool completely.

bite-size coconut macaroons

PREP TIME: 20 minutes
COOK TIME: 15 minutes
YIELD: 12 cookies

TOOLS/EQUIPMENT

- Baking sheet
- Parchment paper (optional)
- Food processor
- Large bowl
- Whisk or fork
- Wire rack

Butter, for greasing the baking
   sheet (optional)
2 cups sweetened flaked coconut
2 large egg whites
¼ cup granulated sugar
½ teaspoon vanilla extract
⅛ teaspoon table salt

Preheat the oven to 350°F.
Lightly grease a baking sheet or line with parchment paper.

Chop the coconut.
Place the coconut in a food processor, and pulse until finely chopped.

Whisk the ingredients.
In a large bowl, whisk together the egg whites, sugar, vanilla, and salt until well blended. Stir in the coconut.

Bake the macaroons.
Drop the coconut mixture, about 2 teaspoons each, onto the prepared baking sheet, leaving about 2 inches between cookies. Bake for 10 to 15 minutes, or until golden brown around the edges. Cool for a few minutes, then transfer the cookies to a wire rack to finish cooling.

TRY INSTEAD: Instead of vanilla extract, try a different extract like almond or orange.

HELPFUL HINT: You don't have to chop the coconut, but I prefer smaller pieces. You can also chop the coconut with a knife on a cutting board.

FOOD FACT: The white, fleshy part of the coconut seed is called coconut meat.

vanilla tuiles

PREP TIME: 20 minutes
(plus 2 hours chill time)
COOK TIME: 10 minutes
YIELD: 24 cookies

TOOLS/EQUIPMENT

- Large bowl
- Whisk or fork
- Plastic wrap
- Baking sheets
- Parchment paper (optional)
- Offset spatula or butter knife

¾ cup granulated sugar

3 large egg whites

½ cup (1 stick) unsalted butter, melted and cooled

1 teaspoon vanilla extract

½ cup all-purpose flour

⅛ teaspoon table salt

Butter, for greasing the baking sheets (optional)

Mix all the ingredients.
In a large bowl, whisk together the sugar and egg whites until well blended. Whisk in the melted butter and vanilla until well blended, then beat in the flour and salt until just combined.

Refrigerate the batter.
Cover the bowl with plastic wrap and refrigerate at least 2 to 3 hours or overnight.

Preheat the oven to 350°F.
But first, position an oven rack in the middle of the oven. Grease baking sheets or line them with lightly greased parchment paper.

Form the cookies.
Spoon about 2 teaspoons of batter onto prepared baking sheets. With an offset spatula or the back of a spoon, spread the batter into a very thin circle, 3 to 4 inches wide. Repeat, leaving about an inch of space between cookies.

Bake the cookies.
Bake for 7 to 10 minutes, or until golden brown around the edges. Cool for a few seconds, then remove from the pan and quickly roll the cookies into tubes before they cool (see Helpful Hint). Cool completely.

> **HELPFUL HINT:** The cookies harden quickly so only bake a few cookies at a time, and make sure your pan is completely cool before placing a new batch on the pan.

honey roasted peanut butter cookies

PREP TIME: 20 minutes (plus 30 minutes chill time)
COOK TIME: 17 minutes
YIELD: 24 cookies

TOOLS/EQUIPMENT

- Medium bowl
- Large bowl
- Electric hand mixer
- Plastic wrap
- 2 baking sheets
- Parchment paper (optional)
- Fork
- Wire rack

2¾ cups all-purpose flour

1¼ teaspoons baking soda

¼ teaspoon table salt

¾ cup (1½ sticks) unsalted butter, at room temperature

¼ cup shortening

1¼ cups brown sugar

½ cup plus 1 tablespoon granulated sugar, divided

1 cup creamy peanut butter

2 large eggs, at room temperature

2 teaspoons vanilla extract

1 cup chopped honey roasted peanuts

Mix the dry ingredients.
In a medium bowl, stir together the flour, baking soda, and salt.

Cream the butter and sugar.
In a large bowl, beat the butter and shortening with an electric mixer on medium speed for about 10 seconds, or until smooth. Beat in the brown sugar and ½ cup of granulated sugar until well blended and light and fluffy, about 2 minutes. Beat in the peanut butter, then beat in the eggs one at a time, beating after each addition. Beat in the vanilla until well blended.

Mix the ingredients.
Beat the flour mixture into the butter and sugar mixture until just combined. With a spoon, stir in the nuts.

Refrigerate the dough.
Cover the dough with plastic wrap and refrigerate for a half-hour or more, until firm.

Preheat the oven to 375°F.

Bake the cookies.
Drop the cookie dough in big (3-tablespoon) lumps onto ungreased baking sheets or baking sheets lined with parchment paper, leaving about 2 inches between cookies. Gently press down on the cookies with a fork (up and down, and side to side) to make a crisscross pattern. Sprinkle lightly with the remaining tablespoon of sugar. Bake for 13 to 17 minutes, or until golden brown around the edges, rotating the pans halfway through baking. Cool slightly, then transfer the cookies to a wire rack to cool completely.

TRY INSTEAD: Instead of chopped peanuts, substitute your favorite chocolate chip!

DID YOU KNOW? Peanut allergies can be very serious—even life threatening. Be sure to check with people if they have a nut allergy before serving.

thick and chewy chocolate chip cookies

PREP TIME: 30 minutes
(plus 2 hours chill time)
COOK TIME: 18 minutes
YIELD: 30 cookies

TOOLS/EQUIPMENT

- Medium bowl
- Large bowl
- Electric hand mixer
- Plastic wrap
- 2 baking sheets
- Parchment paper (optional)
- Wire rack

3⅓ cups all-purpose flour
1 tablespoon cornstarch
1 teaspoon baking powder
1 teaspoon baking soda
1 teaspoon table salt
1 cup (2 sticks) unsalted butter, melted and cooled slightly
1 cup brown sugar
1 cup granulated sugar
1 large egg
2 large egg yolks
1 teaspoon vanilla extract
1 (12-ounce) bag mini chocolate chips

Mix the dry ingredients.
In a medium bowl, stir together the flour, corn-starch, baking powder, baking soda, and salt.

Cream the butter and sugar.
In a large bowl, beat the melted butter, brown sugar, and granulated sugar with an electric mixer on medium speed until well blended and light and fluffy, about 2 minutes. Beat in the egg and egg yolks, then beat in vanilla until well blended.

Beat the ingredients.
Add the flour mixture to the butter and sugar mixture, and beat with an electric mixer on medium speed until blended. With a spoon, stir in the chocolate chips.

Refrigerate the dough.
Drop the dough in large (3-tablespoon) lumps on a large baking sheet or 2 baking sheets, leaving about 2 inches between cookies. Cover the dough with plastic wrap and refrigerate at least 2 hours or overnight. »

TRY INSTEAD: Instead of mini chocolate chips, use another favorite—white chocolate, butterscotch, or peanut butter chips all work!

HELPFUL HINT: A large trigger ice cream scoop helps make cookies the same size. Flatten the cookies slightly before baking if using an ice cream scoop.

TROUBLESHOOTING TIP: The melted butter should be slightly warm when adding it to other ingredients, but make sure it's not hot. If it's too hot, it may cook the eggs before you bake the cookies!

Preheat the oven to 325°F.

Bake the cookies.
Bake for 15 to 18 minutes on ungreased baking sheets or baking sheets lined with parchment paper, or until lightly browned around the edges, rotating the pans halfway through cooking. Cool slightly, then transfer the cookies to a wire rack to cool completely.

chocolate pecan tassie cookie cups

PREP TIME: 30 minutes
COOK TIME: 30 minutes
YIELD: 24 cookies

TOOLS/EQUIPMENT

- 2 medium bowls
- Electric mixer
- Mini muffin pan (24-cup)
- Wire rack

FOR THE COOKIES

½ cup (1 stick) unsalted butter, at room temperature
⅓ cup (3 ounces) plain cream cheese, at room temperature
1 cup all-purpose flour

FOR THE FILLING

1 large egg
¾ cup brown sugar
1 tablespoon unsalted butter, melted
⅓ cup chopped pecans
⅓ cup mini chocolate chips

Preheat the oven to 325°F.

Make the cookie dough.
In a medium bowl, beat together ½ cup of room-temperature butter and the cream cheese with an electric mixer on medium speed until well blended. Beat in the flour until just blended.

Prepare the filling.
In another medium bowl, whisk together the egg, brown sugar, and melted butter until well blended. Stir in the pecans and chocolate chips.

Form the cookies.
Press a rounded teaspoon of cookie dough in each cup of an ungreased 24-cup mini muffin pan. Press the dough in the middle so it goes up the sides to form a little cookie cup. Spoon the filling into each cookie cup about ¾ full.

Bake the cookies.
Bake for 25 to 30 minutes, or until golden brown and slightly puffed. Cool slightly in the pan, then transfer the cookies to a wire rack to finish cooling.

TRY INSTEAD: Instead of pecans, you can also use walnuts or another favorite nut.

PRO TIP: The handle of a wooden spoon dipped in flour helps shape the cookie dough in the cups before adding the filling.

frosted sugar cookie pops

PREP TIME: 45 minutes
(plus 2 hours chill time)
COOK TIME: 14 minutes
YIELD: 24 cookie pops

TOOLS/EQUIPMENT

- Medium bowl
- Large bowl
- Electric mixer
- Plastic wrap
- 2 baking sheets
- Parchment paper (optional)
- Rolling pin
- Round cookie cutter
- White lollipop sticks
- Wire rack

FOR THE COOKIES

3 cups all-purpose flour
¾ teaspoon baking powder
¼ teaspoon table salt
1 cup (2 sticks) unsalted butter,
    at room temperature
1 cup granulated sugar
1 large egg
1 tablespoon milk (2 percent
    or whole)
1 teaspoon vanilla extract
Butter, for greasing the baking
    sheets (optional)

Mix the dry ingredients.
In a medium bowl, stir together the flour, baking powder, and salt.

Cream the butter and sugar.
In a large bowl, beat 1 cup of butter with an electric mixer on medium speed for about 10 seconds or until smooth. Beat in the granulated sugar until well blended and light and fluffy, about 2 minutes. Beat in the egg, 1 tablespoon of milk, and 1 teaspoon of vanilla until well blended.

Blend the ingredients.
Add the flour mixture to the butter and sugar mixture, and beat with an electric mixer on medium speed until blended.

Refrigerate the dough.
Divide the dough in half, and place each half on a large piece of plastic wrap. Flatten each piece to form a large disk, then wrap tightly with plastic wrap. Refrigerate for at least 2 hours or until firm.

Preheat the oven to 375°F.
Lightly grease 2 baking sheets or line with parchment paper.

Create the pops.
Roll out one piece of dough on a lightly floured surface to ¼-inch thick. Using a 3-inch round cookie cutter, cut out circles. Place the circles on the prepared baking sheets. Gently press a lollipop stick about a half-inch into each cookie from the side. Use cookie dough scraps to cover the stick if it pops through.

FOR THE FROSTING

½ cup (1 stick) unsalted butter,
   at room temperature
4 cups confectioners' sugar
½ teaspoon vanilla extract
3 to 6 tablespoons whole milk
Food coloring (optional)
Sprinkles (optional)

Bake the cookies.

Bake for 9 to 14 minutes, or until golden brown around the edges, rotating the pans halfway through baking. Cool slightly, then transfer the cookies to a wire rack to finish cooling.

Make the frosting.

In a medium bowl, beat ½ cup of butter with an electric mixer for about 10 seconds or until smooth. Gradually beat in the confectioners' sugar and ½ teaspoon vanilla. Add 2 tablespoons of milk and beat until smooth, adding a little more milk, one tablespoon at a time, as needed. Add a few drops of food coloring, if desired. Once cookies are completely cooled, frost them and decorate with sprinkles, if desired.

TRY INSTEAD: Instead of frosting all the cookies the same color, divide the frosting and use a few different colors.

PRO TIP: If you don't have a 3-inch cookie cutter, use a small bowl or glass and cut with a knife around the rim.

classic lemon bars

PREP TIME: 30 minutes
(plus 2 hours chill time)
COOK TIME: 50 minutes
YIELD: 16 bars

TOOLS/EQUIPMENT

- 8-inch square baking pan
- Small bowl
- Large bowl
- Electric mixer
- Whisk or fork
- Zester

FOR THE CRUST

Butter, for greasing the pan
1 cup all-purpose flour
⅛ teaspoon table salt
¾ cup (1½ sticks) unsalted butter,
   at room temperature
¼ cup confectioners' sugar
2 tablespoons brown sugar

FOR THE FILLING

2 large eggs, at room temperature
1 large egg yolk
1 cup granulated sugar
3 tablespoons all-purpose flour
½ teaspoon freshly grated
   lemon zest
½ cup freshly squeezed lemon
   juice (3 or 4 lemons)

FOR THE GARNISH

2 tablespoons confectioners'
   sugar

Preheat the oven to 350°F.
Lightly grease an 8-inch square baking pan.

Mix the dry ingredients.
In a small bowl, stir together 1 cup of flour and the salt.

Cream the butter and sugar.
In a large bowl, beat the butter with an electric mixer on medium speed for about 10 seconds, or until smooth. Beat in ¼ cup of confectioners' sugar and the brown sugar until well blended and light and fluffy, about 2 minutes. Add the flour mixture to the butter mixture until just combined. Press the dough evenly onto the bottom of the pan and about ½ inch up the sides of the pan to form the crust.

Bake the crust.
Bake for 15 to 20 minutes, or until golden brown around the edges.

Prepare the filling.
Meanwhile, in a large bowl whisk together the eggs, egg yolk, granulated sugar, 3 tablespoons of flour, lemon zest, and lemon juice until well blended.

Bake the bars.
Remove the crust from the oven and reduce the oven temperature to 300°F. Pour the filling over the cooked crust. Bake for 25 to 30 minutes, or until the filling appears set (firm). Cool the bars, then refrigerate for at least 2 to 3 hours, or until firm enough to cut into bars. Dust with 2 table-spoons of confectioners' sugar before serving.

strawberry cheesecake bars

PREP TIME: 15 minutes
(plus 3 hours chill time)
COOK TIME: 40 minutes
YIELD: 16 bars

TOOLS/EQUIPMENT

- 8-inch square baking pan
- 2 medium bowls
- Electric mixer
- Blender

FOR THE CRUST

Butter, for greasing the pan
1½ cups graham cracker crumbs
    (10 to 12 whole graham
    crackers)
4 tablespoons unsalted butter,
    melted

FOR THE CHEESECAKE

2 (8-ounce) bricks cream cheese,
    at room temperature
½ cup granulated sugar
2 large eggs, at room temperature
½ teaspoon vanilla extract

FOR THE STRAWBERRY SAUCE

1 pound frozen strawberries,
    thawed
¼ cup granulated sugar
1 teaspoon vanilla extract

Preheat the oven to 350°F.
Lightly grease an 8-inch square baking pan.

Prepare the crust.
In a medium bowl, mix together the graham cracker crumbs and melted butter. Press the mixture evenly into the bottom of the pan.

Make the cheesecake.
In another medium bowl, beat the cream cheese with an electric mixer on medium speed until smooth. Beat in ½ cup of sugar until well blended. Beat in the eggs one at a time, beating after each addition, then beat in ½ teaspoon of vanilla. Pour the mixture over the crust.

Bake the cheesecake.
Bake for 30 to 40 minutes, or until center is almost set (firm). Let cool, then refrigerate at least 3 hours, or overnight, until fully chilled.

Make the strawberry sauce.
Meanwhile, in a blender, add the thawed strawberries, ¼ cup of granulated sugar, and 1 teaspoon of vanilla. Pulse repeatedly until smooth.

Serve the treat.
Once the cheesecake is fully chilled, cut it into bars, and drizzle with a little strawberry sauce before serving.

HELPFUL HINT: You can use a food processor instead of a blender to make the strawberry sauce. If you like your sauce really smooth, pour the sauce through a fine mesh strainer to get any seeds out.

PRO TIP: Thawed frozen berries work well for making quick sauces, because they are soft and full of liquid.

TROUBLESHOOTING TIP: Cheesecake is best served the next day. So, if you're having a hard time cutting it into bars, make sure it is fully chilled.

no campfire s'mores bars

PREP TIME: 20 minutes

COOK TIME: 30 minutes

YIELD: 16 bars

TOOLS/EQUIPMENT

- 8-inch square baking pan
- Medium bowl
- Large bowl
- Electric hand mixer
- Spatula
- Wax or parchment paper

Butter, for greasing the pan

1¼ cups all-purpose flour

¾ cup graham cracker crumbs
(5 or 6 whole graham crackers)

½ teaspoon baking soda

½ teaspoon table salt

1 cup (2 sticks) unsalted butter,
at room temperature

¾ cup granulated sugar

¾ cup brown sugar

1 large egg

1 teaspoon vanilla extract

4 (1½-ounce) milk chocolate
candy bars

1 (7½-ounce) jar marshmallow
crème (Marshmallow Fluff)

Preheat the oven to 350˚F.

Lightly grease an 8-inch square baking pan.

Mix the dry ingredients.

In a medium bowl, stir together the flour, graham cracker crumbs, baking soda, and salt.

Cream the butter and sugar.

In a large bowl, beat the butter with an electric mixer on medium speed for about 10 seconds, or until smooth. Beat in the granulated sugar and brown sugar on medium speed until well blended and light and fluffy, about 2 minutes. Beat in the egg, then add the vanilla, beating until well blended.

Beat the ingredients.

Add the flour mixture to the butter and sugar mixture, and beat on medium speed until blended.

Form the cookies.

Spread half of the cookie batter on the bottom of the pan, using your fingers or the back of a fork to evenly cover the pan. Place the chocolate bars on top of the dough in a single layer, breaking the bars into pieces as necessary to fit. Using a spatula, spread the marshmallow crème on top of the chocolate in an even layer. Press the remaining cookie dough on a large sheet of wax or parchment paper to form an 8-inch square. Flip the cookie dough over on top of the marshmallow crème, and remove the paper. »

Bake the cookies.

Bake for 25 to 30 minutes, or until golden brown around the edges. Cool completely before cutting into bars.

TRY INSTEAD: Instead of plain chocolate bars, you can use a 12-ounce bag of milk chocolate chips or other kinds of chocolate bars.

HELPFUL HINT: To make graham cracker crumbs, place graham crackers into a resealable plastic bag. Roll over the bag with a rolling pin a few times until the crackers are crushed into crumbs. You can also use a food processor.

TROUBLESHOOTING TIPS: Marshmallow crème can be difficult to spread over chocolate. Spoon small scoops of the fluff all over the chocolate, then gently spread in each little area.

oat pear bars

PREP TIME: 30 minutes

COOK TIME: 40 minutes

YIELD: 16 bars

TOOLS/EQUIPMENT

- 8-inch square baking pan
- Medium bowl
- Large bowl
- Electric mixer
- Small saucepan
- Slotted spoon

Butter, for greasing the pan

¾ cup all-purpose flour

¾ cup old-fashioned rolled oats

½ teaspoon baking powder

½ teaspoon table salt

3 tablespoons unsalted butter, melted and cooled

½ cup brown sugar

1 large egg yolk

½ teaspoon vanilla extract

2 cups peeled, cored, and finely chopped pear (2 or 3 pears)

3 tablespoons maple syrup

Preheat the oven to 350°F.

Lightly grease an 8-inch square baking pan.

Mix the dry ingredients.

In a medium bowl, stir together the flour, oats, baking powder, and salt.

Cream the butter and sugar.

In a large bowl, beat together the melted butter and brown sugar with an electric mixer on medium speed until well blended and light and fluffy, about 2 minutes. Beat in the egg yolk, then beat in the vanilla.

Combine the ingredients.

Beat the flour mixture into the butter and sugar mixture until just combined.

Bake the crust.

Spread about ⅔ of the cookie batter evenly over the bottom of the prepared pan. Using your fingers or the back of a fork, press down to make an even layer. Bake the crust for 10 to 15 minutes, or until slightly puffed and golden brown around the edges.

Cook the pears.

Meanwhile, in a small saucepan over medium heat, heat the chopped pears and maple syrup. Cook for 5 to 7 minutes, or until the pears begin to soften.

Bake the bars.

Remove the crust from the oven. With a slotted spoon, spoon the pears over the top of the crust. Sprinkle the remaining cookie batter on top. Bake for 15 to 20 minutes, or until the edges are slightly browned. Cool completely before cutting into bars.

chocolate chunk brownies

PREP TIME: 20 minutes
COOK TIME: 30 minutes
YIELD: 16 brownies

TOOLS/EQUIPMENT
- 8-inch square baking pan
- Double boiler (or Make Your Own Double Boiler, page 53)
- Small bowl
- Large bowl
- Whisk

Butter, for greasing the pan
1 (12-ounce) bag semisweet chocolate chips, divided
½ cup (1 stick) unsalted butter
⅓ cup all-purpose flour
¾ teaspoon baking powder
¼ teaspoon table salt
½ cup granulated sugar
2 large eggs, at room temperature
1 teaspoon vanilla extract
1 cup chopped pecans or walnuts

Preheat the oven to 350°F.
Lightly grease an 8-inch square baking pan.

Melt the chocolate.
In the top of a double boiler, combine 1 cup of chocolate chips and the butter. Place over boiling water, then reduce the heat to low. Stir constantly until the chocolate and butter are melted and smooth. Remove from heat and let cool completely, 30 to 45 minutes.

Mix the dry ingredients.
In a small bowl, stir together the flour, baking powder, and salt.

Whisk additional ingredients.
In a large bowl, whisk together the sugar, eggs, and vanilla until well blended.

Combine the ingredients.
Slowly whisk the cooled chocolate mixture into the egg mixture until well blended, then stir in the flour mixture until just combined. Stir in the remaining chocolate chips and nuts.

Bake the brownies.
Pour the batter into the baking pan, spreading evenly. Bake 25 to 30 minutes, or until almost set in middle. Cool completely before cutting into bars.

> TROUBLESHOOTING TIP: Underbake these fudgy brownies just slightly, because they can burn around the edges quickly!

white chocolate blondies

PREP TIME: 20 minutes
COOK TIME: 30 minutes
YIELD: 16 blondies

TOOLS/EQUIPMENT

- 8-inch square baking pan
- Medium bowl
- Large bowl
- Electric mixer

Butter, for greasing the pan
1 cup all-purpose flour
½ teaspoon baking powder
¼ teaspoon baking soda
½ teaspoon table salt
5 tablespoons unsalted butter,
    at room temperature
¾ cup light brown sugar
1 large egg
1 large egg yolk
1 teaspoon vanilla extract
1 cup white chocolate chips

Preheat the oven to 350°F.
Lightly grease an 8-inch square baking pan.

Mix the dry ingredients.
In a medium bowl, stir together the flour, baking powder, baking soda, and salt.

Cream the butter and sugar.
In a large bowl, beat the butter with an electric mixer on medium speed for about 10 seconds, or until smooth. Beat in the brown sugar until well blended and light and fluffy, about 2 minutes. Beat in the egg and egg yolk, then beat in the vanilla until well blended.

Beat the ingredients.
Add the flour mixture to the butter and sugar mixture, and beat with an electric mixer on medium speed until blended. With a spoon, stir in the white chocolate chips.

Bake the blondies.
Pour the batter into the prepared pan. Bake for 25 to 30 minutes, or until light golden brown around the edges. Cool completely before cutting into bars.

TRY INSTEAD: Instead of white chocolate chips, you could use your favorite chip and/or chopped nuts!

DID YOU KNOW? Toss the chips in a little flour before adding them to the batter to prevent them from sinking.

6

pies, tarts & pastries

baked peach hand pies

PREP TIME: 45 minutes (plus 30 minutes chill time)

COOK TIME: 30 minutes

YIELD: 16 pies

TOOLS/EQUIPMENT

- 2 baking sheets
- Parchment paper
- Small saucepan
- Plastic wrap
- Rolling pin
- 4-inch round cookie cutter (optional)
- Pastry brush
- Slotted spoon
- Wire rack

FOR THE PIE

1 Pie Dough (page 45)
3½ cups peeled, finely
  chopped fresh ripe peaches
  (3 or 4 peaches)
¼ cup granulated sugar
½ teaspoon vanilla extract
¼ teaspoon cinnamon
⅛ teaspoon table salt
Flour, for dusting the work surface

FOR THE EGG WASH

1 large egg, beaten
1 teaspoon granulated sugar

Chill the pie dough.

Refrigerate the pie dough while preparing the other ingredients, so it will be easier to handle.

Preheat the oven to 450°F.

Line 2 baking sheets with parchment paper.

Prepare the peach filling.

In a small saucepan over medium heat, heat the chopped peaches, ¼ cup of sugar, vanilla, cinnamon, and salt. Cook for 7 to 10 minutes, stirring occasionally, until the mixture is thickened and the peaches are soft. Spoon into a small bowl, cover with plastic wrap, and refrigerate until completely cool, about 30 minutes.

Form the crust.

Meanwhile, roll out half of the chilled pie dough on a lightly floured surface, to about ⅛ inch thick. Cut out 4-inch circles. Gather the dough scraps, roll out again, and cut out more rounds. Repeat with the remaining dough. Place the rounds on prepared baking sheets.

Assemble the pies.

Lightly brush the outside rim of each crust round with a little beaten egg. With a slotted spoon, spoon about 2 teaspoons of cooled peach filling in the center of each round. Fold the rounds over into half-circles, and press the seams together to seal. Brush the tops with a little more beaten egg, and sprinkle the remaining teaspoon of sugar on top of the pies.

Bake the pies.

Bake for 16 to 20 minutes or until puffed and golden brown, rotating the pans halfway through baking. Cool slightly, then transfer the pies to a wire rack to finish cooling.

TRY INSTEAD: What's in season? Instead of peach, try other fruit such as apricots, nectarines, or plums.

HELPFUL HINT: Rolling out the dough on a nonstick mat makes it easy to pick up the rounds after they're cut.

DID YOU KNOW? You can use the back of a fork to seal the seams together— and make a fun pattern doing so!

key lime pie bites

PREP TIME: 20 minutes
(plus 3 hours chill time)

COOK TIME: 20 minutes

YIELD: 16 bars

TOOLS/EQUIPMENT

- 8-inch square baking pan
- 2 medium bowls
- Zester
- Electric mixer

FOR THE CRUST

Butter, for greasing the pan

1 cup graham cracker crumbs
(7 or 8 whole graham crackers)

3 tablespoons unsalted butter,
melted

FOR THE FILLING

3 large egg yolks

1 teaspoon freshly grated key
lime zest

1 (14-ounce) can sweetened
condensed milk

½ cup freshly squeezed key lime
juice

Preheat the oven to 350°F.
Lightly grease an 8-inch square baking pan.

Make the crust.
In a medium bowl, mix together the graham cracker crumbs and melted butter. Press the mixture evenly into the bottom of the pan.

Make the filling.
In a medium bowl, beat the egg yolks and lime zest with an electric mixer about 2 minutes, or until frothy. Beat in the condensed milk, and then the lime juice, until well blended and thickened.

Bake the bars.
Pour the filling over the crust. Bake for 15 to 20 minutes, or until set. Cool completely, then refrigerate for 3 to 4 hours, or until completely chilled.

> TRY INSTEAD: If you can't find key limes, you can substitute limes or bottled key lime juice. You can also freeze this pie for a nice frozen dessert!

> HELPFUL HINT: These Key Lime Pie Bites can be pretty tart, depending on your limes. Sweeten the deal with a garnish of confectioners' sugar, whipped cream and/or quartered key lime slices.

old-fashioned strawberry pie

PREP TIME: 45 minutes (plus
2 hours and 20 minutes chill time)

COOK TIME: 20 minutes

YIELD: 1 pie (serves 8)

TOOLS/EQUIPMENT

- Rolling pin
- 9-inch pie pan
- Parchment paper and/or aluminum foil
- Pie weights or dried beans (optional)
- Blender
- Large saucepan
- Whisk or fork

Flour, for dusting the work surface

1 chilled Pie Dough (page 45)

7 cups fresh strawberries, stems removed and sliced, divided

⅔ to 1 cup water

¾ cup granulated sugar

3 tablespoons cornstarch

Prepare the pie crust.

Roll out the chilled pie dough on a lightly floured surface to about ¼ inch thick. Transfer the dough to a 9-inch pie pan. Trim the extra dough around the edges, and crimp or flute the edges as desired (see Pie Fluting: How To, page 43). Refrigerate for at least 20 to 30 minutes, or until cold.

Preheat the oven to 375°F.

Blind bake the crust.

Line the crust with parchment paper or aluminum foil. Top with pie weights or dried beans, if using. Lightly cover the outer rim of the crust with aluminum foil to prevent over-browning. Bake for 15 to 20 minutes, or until very light golden brown. Remove the pie weights or beans and paper or foil from the crust. Lightly poke any air bubbles that may have formed around the crust to flatten the dough. Set aside to cool.

Blend some berries.

Place 1 cup of strawberries and ⅔ cup of water in a blender, and process until smooth. Add more water as needed so you have 1½ cups of berry mixture. ≫

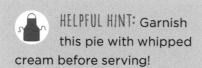

HELPFUL HINT: Garnish this pie with whipped cream before serving!

TROUBLESHOOTING TIP: Be sure to chill the pie completely before slicing so the glaze and pie can set.

Make the glaze.

In a large saucepan, whisk together the sugar and cornstarch. Whisk in the blended berry mixture. Place the saucepan over medium-high heat. Cook for 5 to 7 minutes, stirring, until bubbly and thickened. Remove from the heat to cool.

Assemble the pie.

Spread about ¼ cup of glaze over the bottom and sides of the pie crust. Add the remaining whole strawberries into the pan with the glaze, stir to mix, then spoon the blended strawberries over the glaze in the pie crust into an even layer. Place the pie in the refrigerator for 2 to 3 hours, or until completely chilled.

double-crust blueberry pie

PREP TIME: 20 minutes
COOK TIME: 60 minutes
YIELD: 1 pie (serves 8)

TOOLS/EQUIPMENT

- Large bowl
- Zester
- 9-inch pie pan
- Rolling pin
- Pastry brush
- Baking sheet

4 cups fresh blueberries
½ cup granulated sugar, plus
    1 tablespoon for the topping
½ cup all-purpose flour
1 teaspoon freshly grated
    lemon zest
2 tablespoons freshly squeezed
    lemon juice (about 1 lemon)
Flour, for dusting the work surface
2 chilled Pie Doughs (page 45)
1 egg, lightly beaten

Preheat the oven to 400°F.

Prepare the filling.
In a large bowl, gently stir together the blueberries, ½ cup of sugar, the flour, lemon zest, and lemon juice until blended.

Form the crusts.
Roll out each prepared chilled pie dough crust on a lightly floured surface to about ¼-inch thick. Gently transfer one to a 9-inch pie pan. Cut off any excess dough around edges.

Assemble the pie.
Spoon the blueberry mixture over the dough in the pie pan. Gently place the second dough on top. Press the edges together with a fork or crimp or flute as desired to form a nice seal (see Pie Fluting: How To, page 43). With a pastry brush, brush a little beaten egg over the crust, then cut 3 to 5 slits in the top pie crust with a sharp knife. Sprinkle 1 tablespoon of sugar on top.

Bake the pie.
Place the pie on a baking sheet. Bake for 45 to 60 minutes, or until the pie is golden brown and the filling is bubbly. Cool completely before slicing and serving.

> PRO TIP: The slits in the top pie crust allow the steam to escape while the pie is baking. You can also cut out small shapes instead of slits—use a fun-shaped small cookie cutter if you like!

caramel apple streusel pie

PREP TIME: 30 minutes

COOK TIME: 60 minutes

YIELD: 1 pie (serves 8)

TOOLS/EQUIPMENT

- Small bowl
- Pastry cutter (see Cutting in Butter, page 42)
- Large bowl
- Rolling pin
- 9-inch pie pan
- Aluminum foil
- Baking sheet

FOR THE STREUSEL CRUMB TOPPING

½ cup all-purpose flour

¼ cup brown sugar

½ teaspoon cinnamon

⅛ teaspoon table salt

4 tablespoons cold unsalted butter, cubed

FOR THE PIE

½ cup thick caramel ice cream topping

3 tablespoons all-purpose flour

¼ teaspoon cinnamon

¼ teaspoon table salt

6 cups peeled, thinly sliced cooking apples such as Granny Smith (about 2¼ pounds or 4 to 5 large apples)

1 chilled Pie Dough (page 45)

Flour, for dusting the work surface

Preheat the oven to 375°F.

Make the streusel.

In a small bowl, mix together ½ cup of flour, brown sugar, ½ teaspoon of cinnamon, and ⅛ teaspoon of salt until well blended. With a pastry cutter or the back of a fork, cut in the cold butter cubes until it forms coarse crumbs.

Prepare the apple filling.

In a large bowl, whisk together the caramel topping, 3 tablespoons of flour, ¼ teaspoon of cinnamon, and ¼ teaspoon of salt until well blended. Gently stir in the apples until blended.

Form the crust.

Roll out the chilled pie dough on a lightly floured surface to about ¼-inch thick. Transfer to a 9-inch pie pan. Cut off the excess dough around the edges of the pan.

Make the pie.

Spoon the apples into the pie crust. Sprinkle streusel over the top. Flute or crimp the pie crust as desired (see Pie Fluting: How To, page 43). Cover the edges of the pie crust with aluminum foil.

Bake the pie.

Place the pie on a baking sheet. Bake for about 40 minutes. Remove the foil from edges, then bake for an additional 20 minutes, or until the apples are soft. Cool before slicing and serving.

TRY INSTEAD: Instead of caramel ice cream topping, you can substitute butterscotch.

DID YOU KNOW? Some apples are better for baking than others. Some good baking apple varieties include Cortland, Fuji, Granny Smith, Jonagold, and Golden Delicious. Try one, or even a combination of varieties, in the pie.

TROUBLESHOOTING TIP: Be sure to slice the apples very thin so they cook all the way through. You can also precook the apples a little in a large skillet with a little butter beforehand to ensure they cook through and get nice and soft.

apple tarte tatin

PREP TIME: 30 minutes
(plus 1 hour chill time)
COOK TIME: 50 minutes
YIELD: 1 tarte Tatin (serves 10)

TOOLS/EQUIPMENT

- Medium bowl
- Pastry cutter (see Cutting in Butter, page 42)
- 10½-inch cast-iron pan or oven-safe skillet
- Plastic wrap
- Spoon or tongs
- Rolling pin
- Sharp knife

FOR THE CRUST

1 cup all-purpose flour

¼ cup granulated sugar

⅛ teaspoon table salt

½ cup (1 stick) cold unsalted butter, cubed

1 large egg yolk

2 to 4 tablespoons ice cold water

Flour, for dusting the work surface

FOR THE FILLING

6 tablespoons unsalted butter

1 cup granulated sugar

1 tablespoon freshly squeezed lemon juice

¼ teaspoon table salt

5 large (or 6 small) baking apples (such as Granny Smith), peeled, cored, and quartered

Make the crust.

In a medium bowl, stir together the flour, ¼ cup of sugar, and ⅛ teaspoon of salt until well blended. With a pastry cutter or the back of a fork, cut in ½ cup of cold butter. Stir in the egg yolk. Stir in the cold water, a little at a time, until the dough comes together. Form the dough into a disk, cover completely with plastic wrap, and refrigerate about 1 hour, or until cold and firm.

Preheat the oven to 425°F.

Prepare the filling.

In a cast-iron pan or oven-safe skillet over medium high-heat, add 6 tablespoons of butter, 1 cup of sugar, lemon juice, and ¼ teaspoon of salt. Stir occasionally until blended and butter has melted. Add the apple quarters. Cook 15 to 20 minutes, stirring and turning the apples occasionally, until the liquid has thickened and darkened in color and the apples are a little soft. Remove from heat. With a spoon or tongs, arrange the apples in a single layer in the pan.

Roll out the dough.

On a lightly floured surface, roll out the dough to a circle 11 or 12 inches across. Place the dough over the apples in the pan, and cut off the excess around the edges. With a sharp knife, cut 3 to 5 slits in the crust. »

Bake the tarte.

Bake for 20 to 30 minutes, or until golden brown. Gently turn the pan upside down onto a serving plate, and release the tarte. Serve tarte warm (as it is traditionally served) or cool before serving.

HELPFUL HINT: The skillet will be hot, so use oven mitts when handling. Also, cast-iron pans are really heavy, so don't hesitate to ask a grown-up for help.

TROUBLESHOOTING TIP: If your apple tarte Tatin sticks to the pan while trying to flip it over, run a butter knife around the edges to loosen.

DID YOU KNOW? The tarte Tatin was said to be created by two French sisters, Caroline and Stephanie Tatin, who owned the Hotel Tatin in a rural town outside of Paris.

chocolate pecan pie squares

PREP TIME: 25 minutes
COOK TIME: 40 minutes
YIELD: 16 bars

TOOLS/EQUIPMENT

- 8-inch square baking pan
- Medium bowl
- Electric mixer
- Large bowl

FOR THE CRUST

Butter, for greasing the pan
¾ cup all-purpose flour
⅛ teaspoon table salt
4 tablespoons unsalted butter,
    at room temperature
2 tablespoons brown sugar

FOR THE FILLING

1 large egg
1 large egg yolk
⅓ cup corn syrup
⅓ cup granulated sugar
1 tablespoon unsweetened cocoa
    powder
1 tablespoon unsalted butter,
    melted
½ teaspoon vanilla extract
⅛ teaspoon table salt
¾ cup chocolate chips
¾ cup coarsely chopped pecans

Preheat the oven to 350°F.
Lightly grease an 8-inch square baking pan.

Make the crust.
In a medium bowl, add the flour, ⅛ teaspoon of salt, 4 tablespoons of room-temperature butter, and brown sugar. Beat with an electric mixer on medium speed until blended and crumbly. Press the crust in an even layer over the bottom of the prepared pan. Bake for 10 to 15 minutes, or until golden brown around the edges.

Make the filling.
Meanwhile, in a large bowl, beat the egg, egg yolk, corn syrup, granulated sugar, cocoa powder, 1 tablespoon of melted butter, vanilla, and ⅛ teaspoon of salt with an electric mixer on medium speed until well blended. With a spoon, stir in the chocolate chips and pecans.

Bake the pie squares.
Remove the crust from the oven, and pour the filling evenly over the top of the crust. Bake for 20 to 25 minutes, or until the middle appears set. Cool completely before cutting into bars.

TRY INSTEAD: Instead of chocolate chips and pecans, use another favorite flavored chip and nut!

HELPFUL HINT: I like to place these in the fridge to get nice and cold before cutting into bars.

coconut custard pie
WITH QUICK STRAWBERRY SAUCE

PREP TIME: 30 minutes (plus 20 minutes chill time)
COOK TIME: 80 minutes
YIELD: 1 pie (serves 8)

TOOLS/EQUIPMENT

- Rolling pin
- 9-inch pie pan
- Parchment paper and/or aluminum foil
- Pie weights or dried beans (optional)
- Large bowl
- Whisk or fork
- Baking sheet
- Blender

FOR THE PIE

Flour, for dusting the work surface
1 chilled Pie Dough (page 45)
¾ cup granulated sugar
1 cup half-and-half
4 tablespoons unsalted butter, melted and cooled
6 large eggs, at room temperature
1 teaspoon vanilla extract
¼ teaspoon table salt
2 cups shredded sweetened coconut

FOR THE STRAWBERRY SAUCE

1 pound frozen strawberries, thawed
¼ cup granulated sugar
1 teaspoon vanilla extract

Prepare the pie crust.
Roll out the chilled prepared pie dough on a lightly floured surface to about ¼-inch thick. Transfer the dough to a 9-inch pie pan. Trim the extra dough around the edges and crimp or flute the edges as desired (see Pie Fluting: How To, page 43). Refrigerate the crust for at least 20 to 30 minutes, or until cold.

Preheat the oven to 375°F.

Blind bake the crust.
Line the cold crust with parchment paper or aluminum foil. Top with pie weights or dried beans to prevent bubbles from forming, if desired. Lightly cover the outside rim of the crust with aluminum foil to prevent over-browning. Bake for 15 to 20 minutes, or until very light golden brown. Leave the foil in place around the pie crust, but remove the paper or foil from the bottom of the crust, and also remove the weights or beans. Lightly poke any air bubbles that may have formed on the crust to flatten them.

Lower the oven temperature to 350°F.

Prepare the pie filling.
In a large bowl, whisk together ¾ cup of sugar, half-and-half, melted butter, eggs, 1 teaspoon of vanilla, and salt until well blended. Stir in the coconut.

Bake the pie.

Place the pie pan on a baking sheet, then pour the filling over the crust. Bake for 45 to 60 minutes, or until the filling appears set and golden brown on top. Remove the pie from the oven, and the foil from the crust. Cool completely.

Make the strawberry sauce.

Meanwhile, in a blender, add the thawed strawberries, ¼ cup of sugar, and 1 teaspoon of vanilla. Pulse repeatedly until smooth.

Drizzle and serve.

Drizzle the sauce over the pie right before serving.

banana cream pie

PREP TIME: 30 minutes
(plus 5 hours chill time)
COOK TIME: 45 minutes
YIELD: 1 pie (serves 8)

TOOLS/EQUIPMENT

- Rolling pin
- 9-inch pie pan
- Parchment paper or aluminum foil
- Pie weights or dried beans (optional)
- Small bowl
- Large saucepan
- Whisk or spoon
- Large bowl

FOR THE PIE

Flour, for dusting the work surface
1 chilled Pie Dough (page 45)
2 large egg yolks
¾ cup granulated sugar
¼ cup cornstarch
¼ teaspoon table salt
3 cups milk (2 percent or whole)
3 tablespoons unsalted butter
1 teaspoon vanilla extract
2 large firm, ripe bananas, thinly sliced

FOR THE WHIPPED CREAM

1½ cups cold heavy whipping cream
2 tablespoons granulated sugar

Prepare the crust.

Roll out the prepared chilled pie dough on a lightly floured surface to about ¼ inch thick. Transfer the dough into a 9-inch pie pan. Trim the extra dough around the edges, and crimp or flute the edges as desired (see Pie Fluting: How To, page 43). Refrigerate for at least 20 to 30 minutes, or until cold.

Preheat the oven to 375˚F.

Blind bake the crust.

Line the crust with parchment paper or aluminum foil. Top with pie weights or dried beans, if desired. Lightly cover the outer rim of the crust with foil to prevent over-browning. Bake for 15 to 20 minutes, or until very light golden brown. Remove the pie weights or beans and paper and foil from the crust. Lightly poke any air bubbles that may have formed in the crust to flatten the dough. Set aside to cool.

Prepare the filling.

In a small bowl, beat the egg yolks, then set aside. In a large saucepan over medium-high heat, whisk together ¾ cup of sugar, the cornstarch, salt, and milk. Whisking frequently, cook until very thick, 10 to 20 minutes. While whisking, spoon a little of the hot milk mixture into the bowl with the eggs. Slowly spoon in more milk until the eggs are warm. Pour the remaining milk mixture and the egg mixture into the saucepan. Bring the mixture to a gentle boil and cook 2 to 3 minutes

TRY INSTEAD: You can substitute a prepared graham cracker crust for the pie crust.

TROUBLESHOOTING: Be sure to cook the filling for a long time on the stovetop—until very thick. Otherwise, the filling won't thicken nicely and may be quite soupy.

FOOD FACT: A cluster of bananas is known as a "hand," and a single banana is known as a "finger."

longer, whisking constantly. Remove the pan from heat, and stir in the butter and vanilla until the butter has melted.

Refrigerate the filling.
Pour the filling into a large bowl, cover with plastic wrap, and refrigerate for at least 30 minutes, or until cold.

Add the banana.
Arrange the banana slices evenly over the bottom of the pan. Pour the custard filling over the bananas.

Make whipped cream.
In a large cold bowl, whip the heavy cream and 2 tablespoons of sugar with an electric mixer on medium-high speed until soft peaks form.

Assemble the pie.
Spread the whipped cream on top of the pie. Refrigerate for 4 to 6 hours or overnight. Serve cold.

southern chocolate walnut pie

PREP TIME: 30 minutes (20 minutes chill time, plus cooling time)
COOK TIME: 65 minutes
YIELD: 1 pie (serves 8)

TOOLS/EQUIPMENT

- Rolling pin
- 9-inch pie pan
- Parchment paper and/or aluminum foil
- Pie weights or dried beans (optional)
- Large bowl
- Whisk or fork
- Baking sheet

Flour, for dusting the work surface
1 chilled Pie Dough (page 45)
¾ cup granulated sugar
½ cup all-purpose flour
¼ cup brown sugar
¼ teaspoon table salt
2 large eggs, at room temperature
½ cup (1 stick) unsalted butter, melted and cooled
1 teaspoon vanilla extract
1¼ cups chopped walnuts
1 cup semisweet chocolate chips

Prepare the pie crust.

Roll out the chilled pie dough on a lightly floured surface to about ¼-inch thick. Transfer the dough to a 9-inch pie pan. Trim the extra dough around the edges, and crimp or flute the edges as desired (see Pie Fluting: How To, page 43). Return to the refrigerator for at least 20 to 30 minutes, or until cold.

Preheat the oven to 375°F.

Blind bake the crust.

Line the crust with parchment paper or aluminum foil. Top with pie weights or dried beans, if using. Lightly cover the outer rim of the crust with aluminum foil to prevent over-browning. Bake for 15 to 20 minutes, or until very light golden brown. Leave the foil in place around the edge of the pie crust, but remove the weights or beans and paper or foil from the bottom of the crust. Lightly poke any air bubbles that may have formed around crust to flatten the dough.

Lower the oven temperature to 325°F.

Prepare the filling.

In a large bowl, whisk together the granulated sugar, flour, brown sugar, and salt until well blended. Whisk in the eggs, melted butter, and vanilla until blended. Stir in the walnuts and chocolate chips.

Bake the pie.
Place the pie pan on a baking sheet, then pour the filling over the crust, spreading the walnuts and chocolate chips to evenly distribute. Bake for about 25 minutes, remove the foil from the crust, then bake an additional 10 to 20 minutes, or until the filling appears set (firm). Cool completely before slicing.

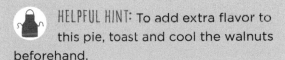

TRY INSTEAD: Instead of semisweet chocolate chips, you can use bitter-sweet or dark chocolate chips.

HELPFUL HINT: To add extra flavor to this pie, toast and cool the walnuts beforehand.

FOOD FACT: This dish is a little different than traditional pecan pie and tastes a little like cookie dough.

homemade pb&j breakfast tarts

PREP TIME: 45 minutes
COOK TIME: 25 minutes
YIELD: 4 tarts

TOOLS/EQUIPMENT

- Rolling pin
- Sharp knife
- Parchment paper (optional)
- Baking sheet
- Pastry brush
- Fork
- Plastic wrap

Flour, for dusting the work surface
Butter, for greasing the pan
   (optional)
1 chilled Pie Dough (page 45)
¼ cup peanut butter
¼ cup jelly
1 large egg, beaten
1 teaspoon granulated sugar

Roll out the dough.

On a lightly floured surface, roll out the chilled pie dough to a 10-by-14-inch rectangle, about ⅛-inch thick.

Cut the dough.

Using a sharp knife, cut out 8 (4-by-3-inch) rectangles. Re-roll the scraps if necessary to get 8 rectangles. Place 4 rectangles on a lightly greased baking sheet or a baking sheet lined with parchment paper, leaving an inch or so between each rectangle.

Fill the dough.

Spread a little peanut butter over the middle of the dough on the baking sheet, leaving about a half-inch border around the edges. Top the peanut butter with the jelly.

Make the tarts.

Lightly brush a little beaten egg around the half-inch dough border. Place the remaining rectangles of dough over the rectangles on the baking sheet. Using the back of a fork, press down around the edges to seal.

Refrigerate the tarts.

Cover lightly with plastic wrap and refrigerate for about 30 minutes, or until chilled.

Preheat the oven to 400˚F.

Bake the tarts.
Brush a little of the remaining egg wash over top of the tarts. Sprinkle with sugar. Bake for 20 to 25 minutes, or until golden brown.

 TRY INSTEAD: Use your favorite flavor of jelly or jam in these tarts!

HELPFUL HINT: If the dough gets too warm and sticky to work with, cover and refrigerate for 20 to 30 minutes.

TROUBLESHOOTING TIP: If you have a hard time cutting the dough into rectangles, cut a piece of 4-by-3-inch paper and use that as your pattern to cut around.

cinnamon sugar palmiers

PREP TIME: 20 minutes (plus 30 minutes chill time)
COOK TIME: 18 minutes
YIELD: 30 palmiers

TOOLS/EQUIPMENT

- 2 baking sheets
- Parchment paper (optional)
- Small bowl
- Rolling pin
- Plastic wrap
- Wire rack

Butter, for greasing the baking sheets (optional)
½ cup granulated sugar
2 teaspoons cinnamon
1 frozen puff pastry sheet (half of a 17-ounce package), thawed according to package directions

Preheat the oven to 400˚F.
Lightly grease 2 baking sheets or line them with parchment paper.

Make the cinnamon sugar.
In a small bowl, mix together the sugar and cinnamon until blended.

Roll out the pastry.
Sprinkle half of the cinnamon-sugar mixture evenly on a large, clean, dry surface. Place the puff pastry on top of the mixture. Sprinkle the rest of the cinnamon-sugar evenly on top of the puff pastry. Using a rolling pin, roll the puff pastry into a 9-by-15-inch rectangle, about ⅛-inch thick.

Form the palmiers.
Starting at the long end of the rectangle, tightly roll up both sides of the dough to meet in the middle. Gently press dough together to stick. Cover the pastry with plastic wrap, and refrigerate 30 to 60 minutes, or until firm.

Slice the palmiers.
Unwrap the chilled pastry. Slice into about ½-inch-thick slices. Place the slices on the prepared baking sheets. »

Bake the palmiers.

Bake for 8 minutes. Remove the palmiers from the oven, flip them over, rotate the pans, then bake an additional 6 to 10 minutes, or until golden brown. Cool slightly, then transfer to a wire rack to finish cooling.

HELPFUL HINT: Puff pastry is a light flaky pastry dough. You can make a homemade version, or it can be found, already made, in the freezer section of your grocery store. Most packages contain 2 sheets. Thaw the puff pastry according to the directions on the package before starting the recipe.

TROUBLESHOOTING TIP: Check on these regularly while they bake. Since the pastry is so thin, it can burn quickly.

FOOD FACT: Palmiers are a French pastry. Palmier is French for "palm" or "palm tree," reflecting their shape.

skillet-baked peach cobbler

PREP TIME: 30 minutes

COOK TIME: 50 minutes

YIELD: 1 cobbler (serves 10)

TOOLS/EQUIPMENT

- 10½-inch cast-iron pan or ovenproof skillet
- Medium bowl
- Large bowl

FOR THE CRUST

6 tablespoons unsalted butter
1 cup all-purpose flour
¾ cup granulated sugar
2 teaspoons baking powder
¼ teaspoon table salt
¾ cup milk (2 percent or whole)

FOR THE FILLING

½ cup brown sugar
1 tablespoon all-purpose flour
1 teaspoon cinnamon
1 tablespoon freshly squeezed orange juice
1 teaspoon vanilla extract
4 cups peeled and sliced fresh ripe peaches (6 to 8 peaches)

Preheat the oven to 375°F.

Melt the butter.
Place the butter in a 10½-inch cast-iron pan or ovenproof skillet. Place the pan in the oven for 3 to 5 minutes, or until the butter is melted. Remove from the oven, and swirl the pan around to form an even layer of melted butter.

Make the crust batter.
Meanwhile, in a medium bowl, mix together 1 cup of flour, the granulated sugar, baking powder, and salt until blended. Stir in the milk.

Create the filling.
In a large bowl, gently stir together the brown sugar, 1 tablespoon of flour, and cinnamon until blended. Stir in the orange juice and vanilla. Gently mix in the peach slices.

Build the cobbler.
Spoon the crust batter over the melted butter in the pan. Spoon the peaches on top.

Bake the cobbler.
Bake for 30 to 45 minutes, or until the crust is golden brown.

mini blueberry peach crostatas

PREP TIME: 30 minutes

COOK TIME: 35 minutes

YIELD: 4 crostatas

TOOLS/EQUIPMENT

- Baking sheets
- Parchment paper (optional)
- Rolling pin
- Large bowl
- Pastry brush

Butter, for greasing the baking sheets (optional)

1 chilled Pie Dough (page 45)

Flour, for dusting the work surface

2 cups peeled, coarsely chopped fresh ripe peaches (3 or 4 peaches)

1 cup fresh blueberries

3 tablespoons granulated sugar, divided

2 teaspoons all-purpose flour

1 teaspoon freshly squeezed lemon juice

1 large egg, beaten

Preheat the oven to 375°F.

Lightly grease baking sheets or line with parchment paper.

Form the crusts.

Divide prepared chilled pie dough into 4 equal balls. Roll out each ball on a lightly floured surface to about ¼-inch thick to form a circle 6 or 7 inches wide. Place the crusts on the baking sheets. Refrigerate the crusts while you make the filling.

Prepare the filling.

In a large bowl, gently stir together the peaches, blueberries, 2 tablespoons of sugar, flour, and lemon juice until blended.

Assemble the crostatas.

With a pastry brush, lightly brush a little beaten egg around the edge of each pie crust. Spoon the peach and blueberry filling into the center of each pie crust, leaving about a half-inch border around the edge. Lift and overlap the edges of the crust just over the edge of the filling so the filling in the center is not completely covered. Lightly brush the crust of the dough with a little more egg, and sprinkle the crust with the remaining tablespoon of sugar. »

Bake the crostatas.

Bake for 25 to 35 minutes, or until golden brown around the edges. Serve warm or at room temperature.

TRY INSTEAD: Instead of peaches, you could substitute other fruit, such as plums, nectarines, or apricots.

HELPFUL HINT: These crostatas are extra delightful with a little ice cream or whipped cream on top!

DID YOU KNOW? Crostatas are a great way to practice handling pie dough, since they are supposed to look rustic and not-so-perfect!

maple pear crisp

PREP TIME: 30 minutes

COOK TIME: 55 minutes

YIELD: serves 8

TOOLS/EQUIPMENT

- Large bowl
- 9-inch pie pan
- Pastry cutter or fork (see Cutting in Butter, page 42)

FOR THE FILLING

5 cups ripe pears, peeled, cored, and thinly sliced (4 or 5 pears)

3 tablespoons maple syrup

1 teaspoon vanilla extract

FOR THE TOPPING

¾ cup old-fashioned rolled oats

¾ cup all-purpose flour

¾ cup brown sugar

1 teaspoon cinnamon

¼ teaspoon table salt

½ cup (1 stick) cold unsalted butter, cubed

Preheat the oven to 350°F.

Make the filling.

In a large bowl, gently stir the pears, maple syrup, and vanilla. Pour into a 9-inch pie pan.

Make the topping.

In a large bowl, stir together the oats, flour, brown sugar, cinnamon, and salt until well blended. Cut in the butter with a pastry cutter or the back of a fork until the mixture resembles coarse crumbs. Crumble the topping over the pears.

Bake the crisp.

Bake for 40 to 55 minutes, or until the pears are soft and the topping is crisp and browned.

 TRY INSTEAD: Instead of pears, you can use apples.

 HELPFUL HINT: Be sure the pears are thinly sliced so the pear can cook through.

chocolate dipped cream puffs
(PROFITEROLES)

PREP TIME: 35 minutes
COOK TIME: 32 minutes
YIELD: 12 cream puffs

TOOLS/EQUIPMENT

- Baking sheet
- Parchment paper (optional)
- Small saucepan
- Wooden spoon
- Medium bowl
- Pastry brush
- Double boiler (or see Make Your Own Double Boiler, page 53)
- Wire rack

Butter, for greasing the baking sheet (optional)
¾ cup water
6 tablespoons unsalted butter
1 teaspoon granulated sugar
¼ teaspoon table salt
¾ cup all-purpose flour
4 large eggs, at room temperature, divided
1½ cups chopped semisweet chocolate or chocolate chips
Whipped cream or ice cream, for serving

Preheat the oven to 400°F.
Lightly grease a baking sheet or line with parchment paper.

Make the dough.
In a small saucepan over medium-high heat, add the water, butter, sugar, and salt. Bring to a boil, stirring occasionally with a sturdy large wooden spoon. Stir in the flour. Stir the dough for 1 to 2 minutes, or until the dough comes together and forms a ball. Remove from heat. Transfer the dough to a medium bowl and cool for 5 to 10 minutes.

Add the eggs.
Add 3 eggs, one at a time, to the dough in the bowl, stirring after each addition. Keep stirring until the eggs are well blended and the dough comes together.

Form the cream puffs.
Spoon the dough (about 1½ tablespoons each) onto the prepared baking sheet. Beat the remaining egg in a small bowl, and brush lightly over tops of cream puffs.

Bake the cream puffs.
Bake for 25 to 30 minutes, or until golden brown and puffed. Cool slightly, then transfer to a wire rack to finish cooling.

Melt the chocolate.

Place the chocolate in the top of a double boiler over boiling water, then reduce the heat to low. Stir constantly until chocolate is melted and smooth. Dip the tops of the cream puffs in the melted chocolate, then place them on the wire rack to cool until the chocolate sets.

Fill the cream puffs.

Before serving, cut the cream puffs in half, stuff them with whipped cream or ice cream, then reassemble and serve immediately.

HELPFUL HINT: Instead of spooning the dough onto the baking sheets, you can use a pastry bag with a large plain tip. A large resealable plastic bag with a corner cut off, or even a trigger ice cream scoop, also works well!

TROUBLESHOOTING TIP: If the egg is too thick to brush, you can add a little water or milk to the beaten egg before brushing over the puffs.

cranberry clafoutis

PREP TIME: 15 minutes
COOK TIME: 60 minutes
YIELD: 1 clafoutis (serves 8)

TOOLS/EQUIPMENT

- 1 deep 9-inch pie pan
- Large bowl
- Electric mixer

Butter, for greasing the pan
1 tablespoon unsalted butter
⅔ cup granulated sugar
3 large eggs, at room temperature
1¼ cup milk (2 percent or whole)
⅛ teaspoon table salt
1 teaspoon vanilla extract
½ cup all-purpose flour
2 cups fresh cranberries

Preheat the oven to 350°F.
Grease a deep 9-inch pie pan with butter.

Combine the ingredients.
In a large bowl, beat the sugar and eggs with an electric mixer on medium speed until well blended and pale yellow, about 2 minutes. Beat in the milk, salt, and vanilla until well blended, then beat in the flour until just combined. The batter will be thin.

Bake the clafoutis.
Pour the batter into the prepared pan. Spoon the cranberries on top. Bake for 45 to 60 minutes, or until golden brown. A toothpick inserted into the middle should come out clean.

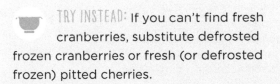

TRY INSTEAD: If you can't find fresh cranberries, substitute defrosted frozen cranberries or fresh (or defrosted frozen) pitted cherries.

HELPFUL HINT: For a nice presentation, serve warm or at room temperature with a little sifted confectioners' sugar on top.

PRO TIP: While the clafoutis cools, the center may fall—this is okay.

chocolate raspberry turnovers

PREP TIME: 30 minutes

COOK TIME: 20 minutes

YIELD: 9 turnovers

TOOLS/EQUIPMENT

- 2 baking sheets
- Parchment paper (optional)
- Small bowl
- Sharp knife
- Pastry brush
- Fork
- Wire rack
- Double boiler (or Make Your Own Double Boiler, page 53)

Butter, for greasing the baking sheets (optional)

¼ cup chopped fresh raspberries

1 tablespoon raspberry jam

¼ teaspoon vanilla extract

1 frozen puff pastry sheet (half of a 17-ounce package), thawed according to package directions

1 large egg, beaten

¾ cup chopped semisweet chocolate or chocolate chips

Preheat the oven to 400°F.

Lightly grease 2 baking sheets or line with parchment paper.

Make the filling.

In a small bowl, stir together the raspberries, jam, and vanilla until blended.

Cut the pastry.

Unfold the puff pastry. With a sharp knife, cut the pastry along the two folds, then cut each piece into 3 equal parts to get 9 pieces in total. Lightly brush the edges with the beaten egg.

Assemble the turnovers.

Spoon about a heaping teaspoon of raspberry filling in the center of each puff pastry. From one corner to the opposite corner, fold the dough over the filling to form a triangle. Using the back of a fork, press down edges of the turnovers to seal.

Bake the turnovers.

Place the turnovers on the prepared baking sheets. Brush the tops of the turnovers lightly with the beaten egg. Bake for 15 to 20 minutes, until puffed and golden brown. Cool slightly, then transfer to a wire rack to finish cooling.

Melt the chocolate.

Place the chocolate in the top of a double boiler over boiling water, then reduce the heat to low. Stir constantly, until the chocolate is melted and smooth. Remove from the heat. With a fork, drizzle the chocolate over the turnovers. Cool until the chocolate sets.

TROUBLESHOOTING TIP: It's okay if a little filling leaks out while the turnovers are baking. With practice, you'll get better at sealing pastry, and besides, these will still taste great!

DID YOU KNOW? An egg wash gives a nice shine and color to baked dough and pastries.

PRO TIP: If you have leftover melted chocolate, spread it on a piece of wax paper. Let the chocolate cool to harden. Then you can break it into pieces and store it in an airtight bag or container for another recipe.

luscious layered chocolate chip bread pudding

PREP TIME: 10 minutes

COOK TIME: 45 minutes

YIELD: 2 (8-ounce) ramekins (serves 2)

TOOLS/EQUIPMENT

- 2 (8-ounce) ramekins
- Baking sheet
- Small bowl
- Whisk or fork

Butter, for greasing the ramekins

2 large eggs, at room temperature

1 cup milk (2 percent or whole)

2 tablespoons granulated sugar

½ teaspoon vanilla extract

⅛ teaspoon table salt

1½ cups cubed day-old fresh bread (about 2 bread slices)

2 tablespoons mini chocolate chips

Preheat the oven to 350°F.

Grease 2 (8-ounce) ramekins with butter and place the ramekins on a baking sheet.

Make the batter.

In a small bowl, whisk together the eggs, milk, sugar, vanilla, and salt until well blended.

Layer the bread pudding.

Place a quarter of the bread cubes into the bottom of each ramekin. Top each with a quarter of the chocolate chips. Top with the remaining bread cubes then the remaining chocolate chips. Slowly pour some of the milk mixture over the bread until the ramekin is about ¾ full. With the back of a fork, gently press down on the bread to soak up some of the liquid. Depending on your bread, you may have extra liquid left; discard any leftovers.

Bake the bread puddings.

Bake for 35 to 45 minutes, or until the puddings appear set (firm) and a toothpick inserted into the middle comes out clean. Serve warm.

TRY INSTEAD: Instead of mini chocolate chips, you can use your favorite chopped chocolate. You can also use 1 cup chocolate milk instead of the milk and sugar.

HELPFUL HINT: Be sure the bread you use is a good-quality day-old bread (or two-day old). Fresh soft bread is already moist so it won't soak up the liquid as well.

mini orange cookie tarts

PREP TIME: 30 minutes (plus 30 minutes chill time)
COOK TIME: 25 minutes
YIELD: 20 tarts

TOOLS/EQUIPMENT

- 2 medium bowls
- Electric hand mixer
- Whisk or fork
- Zester
- Mini muffin pan

FOR THE CRUST

½ cup (1 stick) unsalted butter, at room temperature
½ cup confectioners' sugar
1 cup all-purpose flour
⅛ teaspoon table salt

FOR THE FILLING

½ cup plus 2 tablespoons sweetened condensed milk
¼ cup freshly squeezed orange juice (1 or 2 oranges)
2 tablespoons orange zest
2 large egg yolks
½ teaspoon orange extract
¼ teaspoon vanilla extract

Preheat the oven to 325°F.

Make the cookie crust.
In a medium bowl, beat the butter with an electric mixer on medium speed for about 10 seconds, or until smooth. Add the sugar, beating until well blended and light and fluffy, about 2 minutes. Beat in the flour and salt until just combined.

Make the filling.
In another medium bowl, whisk together the milk, orange juice, zest, yolks, orange extract, and vanilla until well blended.

Form the cookies.
Press a rounded teaspoon of cookie dough in about 20 cups of an ungreased 24-cup mini muffin pan. Press in the center to push the dough up the sides of each pan cup to form a little cookie cup. Spoon about 2 teaspoons of the filling into each cookie cup, or until each cup is about ¾ full.

Bake the cookies.
Bake for 20 to 25 minutes, or until filling is set and cookies are golden brown. Cool slightly in pan, then finish cooling in refrigerator for about 30 minutes, or until chilled.

TRY INSTEAD: The orange extract gives a more intense orange flavor to the tart. If you can't find it, you can substitute an equal amount of vanilla extract instead.

savory baked goods

ham and cheese quiche

PREP TIME: 30 minutes (plus 20 minutes chill time)

COOK TIME: 50 minutes

YIELD: 1 quiche (serves 8)

TOOLS/EQUIPMENT

- Rolling pin
- 9-inch pie pan
- Parchment paper and/or aluminum foil
- Pie weights or dried beans (optional)
- Small bowl
- Large bowl

Flour, for dusting the work surface
1 chilled Pie Dough (page 45)
1 cup chopped ham
½ cup shredded Cheddar cheese
½ cup shredded Swiss cheese
2 tablespoons chopped scallion
4 large eggs
1¼ cups half-and-half or whole milk
1 teaspoon Dijon mustard
½ teaspoon table salt
⅛ teaspoon freshly ground black pepper

Prepare the pie crust.

On a lightly floured surface, roll out the chilled pie dough to about ¼-inch thick. Transfer the dough to a 9-inch pie pan. Trim the extra dough around the edges, and crimp or flute the edges as desired (see Pie Fluting: How To, page 43). Refrigerate for at least 20 to 30 minutes, or until cold.

Preheat the oven to 375°F.

Blind bake the crust.

Line the crust with parchment paper or aluminum foil. Top with pie weights or dried beans, if using. Lightly cover the outer rim of the crust with aluminum foil to prevent over-browning. Bake for 15 to 20 minutes, or until very light golden brown. Remove the pie weights or beans and paper or foil from crust. Lightly poke any air bubbles that may have formed around the crust to flatten the dough. Set aside to cool.

Reduce the oven temperature to 350°F.

Mix the ham and cheese.

In a small bowl, mix together the ham, Cheddar cheese, Swiss cheese, and scallion. Spoon evenly over the pie crust.

Blend remaining ingredients.

In a large bowl, whisk the eggs until well beaten. Beat in the half-and-half or milk, mustard, salt, and black pepper until well blended. Pour the mixture over the ham and cheese in the pie crust.

Bake the quiche.

Bake for 35 to 50 minutes, or until a toothpick or knife inserted near the center comes out clean. Cool about 10 minutes before slicing and serving.

TRY INSTEAD: Quiche is a fun dish to test your creativity. Instead of ham and Swiss and Cheddar cheeses, use any favorite precooked meats and cheeses. You can also substitute or add in finely chopped vegetables such as peppers and onions.

HELPFUL HINT: You can use a store-bought pie crust for quiche. They often come in packages of two, so if you'd like, double the filling recipe.

DID YOU KNOW? Half-and-half can be found in the refrigerated section of your grocery store. It's made of half heavy cream and half milk.

breakfast strata

PREP TIME: 25 minutes
(plus 4 hours chill time)
COOK TIME: 65 minutes
YIELD: serves 8

TOOLS/EQUIPMENT

- 8-inch square baking pan
- Large bowl
- Fork or spatula

Butter, for greasing the pan
4 cups cubed day-old good-
    quality bread (4 or 5 slices)
1 cup precooked, crumbled or
    chopped breakfast sausage
1 cup shredded cheese (such as
    Cheddar or Swiss)
4 large eggs
1 cup milk (2 percent or whole)
1 teaspoon Dijon mustard
¼ teaspoon table salt
⅛ teaspoon freshly ground black
    pepper

Prepare the pan.
Lightly grease an 8-inch square baking pan.

Build the layers.
Add half the bread cubes to the pan. Sprinkle half the sausage and half the cheese on top. Repeat with another layer of bread, sausage, and cheese.

Make the filling.
In a large bowl, whisk the eggs until beaten. Whisk in the milk, mustard, salt, and black pepper until well blended. Pour the mixture in the pan over the bread. Gently press down on the bread with the back of a fork or a spatula to help the bread absorb the liquid.

Refrigerate the strata.
Lightly cover the strata, and refrigerate for at least 4 hours or overnight. Remove the strata from the refrigerator about 30 minutes before baking. (Putting the strata right in the oven can be risky—the sudden change of temperature can cause some pans to crack or break.)

Preheat the oven to 325°F.

Bake the strata.

Bake for 50 to 65 minutes, or until the center appears set and a knife inserted into the center comes out clean. Cool 10 to 15 minutes before cutting and serving.

TRY INSTEAD: Instead of store-bought bread, try the Old-Fashioned White Sandwich Bread (page 78).

PRO TIP: Use a full-fat cheese for best melting. And use any kind of sausage you like, such as pork, turkey, or chicken. I like to use chicken sausage and a shredded Italian cheese blend. You can also add a cup of chopped precooked vegetables.

FOOD FACT: A strata is similar to a bread pudding. It's a dish generally made up of layers of bread, cheese, and meat or vegetables, with a mixture of egg and milk poured over top. It's usually refrigerated for a while before it's baked.

rosemary french cheese puffs
(GOUGÈRES)

PREP TIME: 35 minutes
COOK TIME: 37 minutes
YIELD: 30 puffs

TOOLS/EQUIPMENT

- 2 baking sheets
- Parchment paper (optional)
- Small saucepan
- Wooden spoon
- Medium bowl
- Small bowl
- Pastry brush
- Wire rack

Butter, for greasing the baking
  sheets (optional)
¾ cup water
6 tablespoons unsalted butter
¼ teaspoon table salt
⅛ teaspoon freshly ground black
  pepper
¾ cup all-purpose flour
4 large eggs, at room temperature,
  divided
1 cup grated Gruyère or Swiss
  cheese
2 tablespoons chopped fresh
  rosemary
½ teaspoon Dijon mustard

Preheat the oven to 400˚F.
Lightly grease 2 baking sheets or line with parchment paper.

Make the dough.
In a small saucepan over medium-high heat, heat the water, butter, salt, and black pepper. Bring to a boil, stirring occasionally with a large, sturdy wooden spoon. Stir in the flour. Stir the dough 1 to 2 minutes, or until the dough comes together and forms a ball. Remove from the heat. Place the dough in a medium bowl and cool 5 to 10 minutes.

Add eggs.
Add 3 eggs, one at a time, to the dough in bowl, stirring after each egg. Keep stirring until eggs are well incorporated and the dough comes together.

Add other ingredients.
Stir in the cheese, rosemary, and mustard until well blended.

Make the puffs.
Spoon the dough (about 2 teaspoons each) onto the prepared baking sheets. In a small bowl, beat the remaining egg, and brush lightly over the tops of the puffs.

Bake the puffs.

Bake for 20 to 25 minutes, or until golden brown and puffed. Cool slightly, then transfer to a wire rack to finish cooling.

 TRY INSTEAD: Instead of rosemary, add another favorite fresh herb!

DID YOU KNOW? You can cut these in half and make mini sandwiches with them. Try with your favorite meats or salad, like egg salad or ham salad.

FOOD FACT: This dough is also known as choux pastry, or *pâte à choux*, which is a pastry dough that contains butter, water, flour, and eggs. Instead of using a raising agent such as baking powder or baking soda, the high moisture in the dough causes the steam to puff the pastry. This type of dough is used for a wide variety of recipes, such as these Gougères, profiteroles (cream puffs), éclairs, French crullers, and more.

parmesan garlic knots

PREP TIME: 25 minutes

COOK TIME: 17 minutes

YIELD: 12 knots

TOOLS/EQUIPMENT

- Baking sheet
- Parchment paper (optional)
- Plastic wrap
- Small bowl
- Pastry brush

Butter, for greasing the baking
sheet (optional)

1 prepared Homemade Pizza
Dough (page 51)

3 to 5 small fresh garlic cloves,
peeled and minced

4 tablespoons unsalted butter,
melted

½ teaspoon table salt

½ teaspoon Italian seasoning

¼ cup finely grated Parmesan
cheese

Preheat the oven to 350°F.
Lightly grease a baking sheet or line with parchment paper.

Form the knots.
Divide the pizza dough into 12 pieces. Roll each piece into a long rope 8 to 12 inches long. Tie each rope into a knot, then tuck the ends underneath the knot. Place the knots on the prepared baking sheet. Lightly cover the knots with plastic wrap and place in a warm, dark, draft-free place for a half hour to an hour, or until risen again.

Bake the knots.
Bake for 13 to 17 minutes, or until very light golden brown.

Make the topping.
Meanwhile, in a small bowl, mix together the garlic, melted butter, salt, and Italian seasoning. Brush over the knots, then sprinkle the cheese on top. Bake an additional 3 to 5 minutes, or until the knots are golden brown.

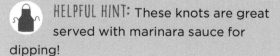 TRY INSTEAD: Instead of Italian seasoning and Parmesan cheese, substitute your favorite dried herbs and cheese.

HELPFUL HINT: These knots are great served with marinara sauce for dipping!

raspberry chipotle brie en croûte

TOOLS/EQUIPMENT
- Small bowl
- Rolling pin
- Pastry brush
- Baking sheet
- Parchment paper (optional)

½ cup raspberry jam
½ teaspoon ground chipotle chile
Flour, for dusting the work surface
1 frozen puff pastry sheet
 (half of a 17-ounce package),
 thawed according to package
 directions
1 large egg, beaten
1 (8-ounce) wheel Brie cheese
¼ cup sliced almonds
Crackers, for serving

Preheat the oven to 375°F.

Make the raspberry chipotle sauce.
In a small bowl, stir together the raspberry jam and chipotle chile until blended.

Wrap the Brie.
On a lightly floured surface, gently roll out the puff pastry to a 12-inch square. Brush the edges of the pastry with the beaten egg. Place the Brie in the center of the pastry. Top the Brie with the raspberry chipotle sauce, then sprinkle the almonds on top. Wrap the sides of the puff pastry up and over the Brie to fully enclose the cheese. Pinch the seams together to seal. Lightly brush the outside of the pastry with the beaten egg.

Bake the Brie.
Place the enclosed brie on an ungreased baking sheet or a baking sheet lined with parchment paper. Bake for 20 to 25 minutes, or until golden brown.

Cut the Brie.
Cut the pastry so the cheese starts to come out. Serve warm with a variety of crackers.

TRY INSTEAD: Instead of raspberry jam, you could also try strawberry or cherry. If nut allergies are a concern, omit the almonds.

pesto straws

PREP TIME: 25 minutes (plus
30 minutes chill time)
COOK TIME: 15 minutes
YIELD: 24 straws

TOOLS/EQUIPMENT

- 2 baking sheets
- Parchment paper (optional)
- Rolling pin
- Spatula
- Plastic wrap

Olive oil, for greasing the baking
    sheets (optional)
Flour, for dusting the work surface
2 frozen puff pastry sheets
    (17-ounce package), thawed
    according to package
    directions
½ cup prepared basil pesto
¼ cup grated Parmesan cheese

DID YOU KNOW? If nut
allergies are a con-
cern, you can substitute a
store-bought or homemade
pesto that does not con-
tain nuts.

Grease the pans.
Lightly grease 2 baking sheets or line with parchment paper.

Roll out the pastry.
On a lightly floured surface, unfold the puff
pastry sheets. Roll out each to a 12-inch square.
Cut each square in half.

Spread the pesto and cheese.
With a spatula, spread the pesto evenly on two of
the pieces of puff pastry, leaving a ¼-inch border.
Sprinkle the cheese over the pesto. Top with the
remaining two pieces of pastry, pressing lightly
around the edges.

Make the straws.
Cut each pastry into 1-inch-wide strips, making
24 straws total. Gently twist each strip, and pinch
the ends of each to seal. Place on the prepared
baking sheets.

Refrigerate the straws.
Lightly cover the straws with plastic wrap, and
refrigerate for at least 30 minutes, or until cold.

Preheat the oven to 400°F.

Bake the straws.
Remove the straws from the refrigerator and
remove the plastic wrap. Bake for 10 to 15 minutes or until golden brown. Cool slightly, then
serve warm.

pepperoni pinwheels

PREP TIME: 30 minutes

COOK TIME: 20 minutes

YIELD: 24 pinwheels

TOOLS/EQUIPMENT

- 2 baking sheets
- Parchment paper (optional)
- Rolling pin
- Sharp knife

Olive oil, for greasing the baking
  sheets (optional)

1 prepared Homemade Pizza
  Dough (page 51)

Flour, for dusting the work surface

⅓ cup tomato sauce

2 cups shredded mozzarella
  cheese

¼ pound thinly sliced pepperoni

Preheat the oven to 375˚F.

Lightly grease 2 baking sheets with olive oil or line with parchment paper.

Roll out the dough.

Divide the dough into 2 even pieces. Roll out each piece of dough on a lightly floured surface to a 10-by-12-inch rectangle.

Make the pinwheels.

Spoon the tomato sauce over each dough rectangle, leaving a ½-inch border. Top the sauce with the cheese, then the pepperoni slices. Starting at the long end, tightly roll up each pizza dough. Pinch along the seam to seal. Using a sharp knife, cut the dough into 1-inch rounds.

Bake the pinwheels.

Place the rounds on baking sheets. Bake for 15 to 20 minutes, or until golden brown.

 HELPFUL HINT: Be sure to roll the dough tightly before slicing.

TROUBLESHOOTING TIP: Deli pepperoni tends to work better than pepperoni that comes in a package because it's larger, making it easier to roll the dough without it falling out.

mini mexican pizzas

PREP TIME: 30 minutes

COOK TIME: 37 minutes

YIELD: 12 pizzas

TOOLS/EQUIPMENT
- 2 baking sheets
- Rolling pin
- Large skillet

Olive oil, for greasing the baking sheets

1 prepared Homemade Pizza Dough (page 51)

Flour, for dusting the work surface

8 ounces ground beef

2 tablespoons taco seasoning

¾ cup plain tomato sauce

2 cups shredded Cheddar cheese

1 cup shredded lettuce

¾ cup finely chopped tomato

¾ cup guacamole

½ cup crushed tortilla chips

Preheat the oven to 375˚F.

Lightly grease 2 baking sheets with olive oil.

Shape the dough.

Divide the pizza dough into 12 balls. On a lightly floured surface, roll out each dough ball into thin circles, 4 or 5 inches wide. Place on the baking sheets.

Precook the dough.

Bake for 10 to 15 minutes, or until just light golden brown.

Brown the beef.

Meanwhile, in a large skillet over medium-high heat, heat the ground beef. Cook, stirring occasionally while breaking up the beef, 5 to 7 minutes, or until thoroughly browned. Drain the grease. Add the taco seasoning to the beef, and stir to combine.

Build the pizzas.

Spoon the tomato sauce on top of each pizza crust, leaving about a ½-inch border around the edges. Sprinkle the cheese over the sauce, then spoon the ground beef on top.

Bake the pizzas.

Bake for 10 to 15 minutes, or until the dough is golden brown and cheese is bubbly.

Top the pizzas.

Top each pizza with the lettuce and tomato. Place a dollop of the guacamole on each pizza and sprinkle with the crushed chips.

sausage and ricotta calzones

PREP TIME: 30 minutes
COOK TIME: 25 minutes
YIELD: 6 calzones

TOOLS/EQUIPMENT

- 2 baking sheets
- Parchment paper (optional)
- Rolling pin
- Large skillet
- Large bowl
- Pastry brush

Olive oil, for greasing the baking
  sheets (optional)
1 prepared Homemade Pizza
  Dough (page 51)
Flour, for dusting the work surface
8 ounces Italian sausage, casings
  removed, crumbled
1 (15-ounce) container ricotta
  cheese
1 large egg
½ teaspoon garlic powder
1 teaspoon dried Italian seasoning
2 cups shredded mozzarella
  cheese
½ cup grated Parmesan cheese
2 tablespoons olive oil
Tomato sauce, for dipping
  (optional)

Preheat the oven to 450°F.
Lightly grease 2 baking sheets with olive oil, or line with parchment paper.

Prepare the pizza dough.
Divide the dough into 6 equal pieces. On a lightly floured surface, roll out each piece of dough to circles about 7 or 8 inches wide.

Cook the sausage.
Meanwhile, in a large skillet over medium-high heat, add the sausage. Cook 5 to 7 minutes, or until cooked through, stirring occasionally while breaking up the sausage. Drain the grease. Set sausage aside to cool.

Make the filling.
In a large bowl, stir together the ricotta cheese, egg, garlic powder, and Italian seasoning until well blended. Stir in the mozzarella cheese, Parmesan cheese, and sausage.

Prepare the calzones.
Spoon about ¾ cup of the cheese and sausage mixture on one side of the dough, leaving about a ½-inch border on the filled side edge. Fold the other side of the dough over the filling, pinching to seal. Starting at one end of the border, fold the border dough over, a little at a time, to secure it into place.

Bake the calzones.
Place the calzones on the prepared baking sheets. Lightly brush olive oil over the calzones. Bake for 20 to 25 minutes or until crust is golden brown, rotating the pans halfway through cooking. Serve with tomato sauce for dipping (optional).

mediterranean phyllo triangles

PREP TIME: 45 minutes
COOK TIME: 20 minutes
YIELD: 30 triangles

TOOLS/EQUIPMENT

- 2 baking sheets
- Large bowl
- Plastic wrap
- Pastry brush

Butter, for greasing the baking sheets

1 (10-ounce) package frozen, chopped spinach, thawed and dried

1 cup crumbled feta cheese

¼ cup chopped oil-packed sun-dried tomatoes, drained

2 large eggs, beaten

3 tablespoons onion, minced

3 garlic cloves, minced

1 tablespoon freshly squeezed lemon juice

1 teaspoon dried oregano

¼ teaspoon table salt

⅛ teaspoon freshly ground black pepper

20 sheets frozen phyllo dough, thawed according to package directions

½ cup (1 stick) unsalted butter, melted

Preheat the oven to 375˚F.
Generously grease 2 baking sheets with butter.

Make the filling.
In a large bowl, mix together the spinach, feta, tomatoes, eggs, onion, garlic, lemon juice, oregano, salt, and black pepper until well blended.

Prepare the phyllo dough.
Unroll the phyllo dough. Cover well with plastic wrap and keep it covered while working. Place one sheet of the dough on a work surface. Gently brush the sheet of dough with melted butter. Place another sheet of dough on top, and brush it with butter. Cut the dough into 3-inch-wide pieces along the long side to make 3 long strips.

Make the triangles.
Spoon about 2 teaspoons of filling on one side of each strip of dough. Take one corner of the strip and fold over the filling to make a triangle. Gently fold again along the strip of dough, and keep going all the way to the end of the strip to make an enclosed triangle. Repeat with the remaining dough until it's all gone. Place the triangles on the prepared baking sheets, brush with more butter, and cover with plastic wrap until ready to bake. »

Bake the triangles.

Remove the plastic wrap and bake for 15 to 20 minutes, or until golden brown, rotating the pans halfway through baking.

HELPFUL HINT: Squeeze the spinach several times to get out as much liquid as possible. Using paper towels or a salad spinner helps. You could also use fresh spinach, just cook and drain it well first.

TROUBLESHOOTING TIP: Phyllo dough can be very delicate and it dries out fast, so be gentle and keep it covered while working with it. Also, avoid rolling the triangles too tightly so they don't crack when baking.

FOOD FACT: Phyllo dough can be found in the freezer section of your grocery store and is different than puff pastry dough. Phyllo dough is a very thin dough that is generally layered to make flaky pastries.

little chicken and mushroom biscuit pot pies

PREP TIME: 40 minutes
COOK TIME: 20 minutes
YIELD: serves 4

TOOLS/EQUIPMENT

- 4 (8-ounce) ramekins
- Baking sheet
- Large skillet
- Medium bowl
- Pastry cutter (see Cutting in Butter, page 42)

FOR THE FILLING

4 tablespoons unsalted butter
1 cup thinly sliced and coarsely chopped mushrooms
¼ cup finely chopped onion
¼ cup finely chopped celery
¼ cup finely chopped carrot
1 garlic clove, minced
¼ cup all-purpose flour
1¼ cups chicken broth
½ cup heavy whipping cream
⅛ teaspoon table salt
⅛ teaspoon freshly ground black pepper
1 cup shredded precooked chicken

FOR THE BISCUIT TOPPING

1 cup all-purpose flour
1 teaspoon baking powder
¼ teaspoon table salt
4 tablespoons cold unsalted butter, cut into small cubes
⅓ cup cold milk (2 percent or whole)

Preheat the oven to 400°F.
Place 4 (8-ounce) ramekins on a baking sheet.

Cook the vegetables.
In a large skillet over medium heat, melt 4 tablespoons of butter. Add the mushrooms, onion, celery, carrot, and garlic. Cook 4 to 5 minutes, or until soft, stirring occasionally.

Finish the filling.
Stir in ¼ cup of flour to the skillet. Once incorporated, slowly stir in the broth and cream until smooth. Cook and stir until thickened and bubbly, 2 to 3 minutes. Stir in ⅛ teaspoon of salt, the black pepper, and shredded chicken. Spoon the mixture into the ramekins.

Make the topping.
In a medium bowl, mix together 1 cup of flour, baking powder, and ¼ teaspoon of salt until well blended. Cut in 4 tablespoons of cold butter with a pastry cutter or the back of a fork until the mixture is crumbly. Mix in the milk, stirring until the dough is just combined. Spoon the biscuit dough in small pieces over the filling in the ramekins.

Bake the pot pies.
Bake for 15 to 20 minutes, or until the biscuit topping is golden brown. Cool slightly before serving.

> **HELPFUL HINT:** Rotisserie chickens from your local grocery store are handy to use for the precooked chicken in this recipe.

BAKING FOR EVERY OCCASION

Now that you've got a collection of great baking recipes, let's talk about when to make them. Some recipes seem to beg to be made for certain occasions; for example, what sleepover would not be complete without Sticky Monkey Bread Bites? Here are some particularly perfect times to consider using these recipes:

For Bake Sales

- Sprinkle Cake Pops (page 86)
- Snickerdoodle Bites (page 116)
- Thick and Chewy Chocolate Chip Cookies (page 127)
- No Campfire S'mores Bars (page 137)
- Bite-Size Coconut Macaroons (page 121)
- Mini Orange Cookie Tarts (page 179)

For Mother's Day

- Yogurt Banana Bread (page 82)
- Lemon Loaf Cake (page 92)
- Classic Lemon Bars (page 132)
- Chocolate Raspberry Turnovers (page 176)
- Ham and Cheese Quiche (page 182)
- Raspberry Chipotle Brie en Croûte (page 190)

For Father's Day

- Cornbread Muffins with Orange Honey Butter (page 65)
- Rosemary Onion Focaccia (page 76)
- White Chocolate Blondies (page 141)
- Strawberry Cheesecake Bars (page 134)
- Mini Blueberry Peach Crostatas (page 168)
- Banana Cream Pie (page 158)

For Breakfast

- Blueberry Muffin Tops with Cheesecake Drizzle (page 63)
- Cinnamon Nut Coffee Cake (page 95)
- Breakfast Strata (page 184)
- Homemade Mini Cheese Bagels (page 74)

For Sleepovers

- Sticky Monkey Bread Bites (page 66)
- Zebra Marble Cake with Vanilla Frosting (page 99)
- Shortbread Dippin' Sticks (page 118)
- Southern Chocolate Walnut Pie (page 160)
- Mini Mexican Pizzas (page 194)
- Pepperoni Pinwheels (page 193)

For Everyday Snacks

- Soft Pretzel Sticks with Honey Mustard Dip (page 68)
- Very Berry Granola Bars (page 27)
- Honey Roasted Peanut Butter Cookies (page 124)
- Pesto Straws (page 191)
- Rosemary French Cheese Puffs (page 186)
- Cinnamon Sugar Palmiers (page 164)

For Chocolate Lovers

- Mini Triple Chocolate Muffins (page 60)
- Chocolate Chunk Brownies (page 140)
- Chocolate Pecan Pie Squares (page 155)
- Luscious Layered Chocolate Chip Bread Pudding (page 178)
- Dark Chocolate Fudge Lava Cakes (page 106)
- Chocolate Pecan Tassie Cookie Cups (page 129)

Appendix B

CONVERSION CHARTS

Volume Equivalents (Liquid)

US STANDARD	US STANDARD (OUNCES)	METRIC (APPROXIMATE)
2 tablespoons	1 fl. oz.	30 mL
¼ cup	2 fl. oz.	60 mL
½ cup	4 fl. oz.	120 mL
1 cup	8 fl. oz.	240 mL
1½ cups	12 fl. oz.	355 mL
2 cups or 1 pint	16 fl. oz.	475 mL
4 cups or 1 quart	32 fl. oz.	1 L
1 gallon	128 fl. oz.	4 L

Volume Equivalents (Dry)

US STANDARD	METRIC (APPROXIMATE)
⅛ teaspoon	0.5 mL
¼ teaspoon	1 mL
½ teaspoon	2 mL
¾ teaspoon	4 mL
1 teaspoon	5 mL
1 tablespoon	15 mL
¼ cup	59 mL
⅓ cup	79 mL
½ cup	118 mL
⅔ cup	156 mL
¾ cup	177 mL
1 cup	235 mL
2 cups or 1 pint	475 mL
3 cups	700 mL
4 cups or 1 quart	1 L

Oven Temperatures

FAHRENHEIT (F)	CELSIUS (C) (APPROXIMATE)
250°F	120°C
300°F	150°C
325°F	165°C
350°F	180°C
375°F	190°C
400°F	200°C
425°F	220°C
450°F	230°C

Weight Equivalents

US STANDARD	METRIC (APPROXIMATE)
½ ounce	15 g
1 ounce	30 g
2 ounces	60 g
4 ounces	115 g
8 ounces	225 g
12 ounces	340 g
16 ounces or 1 pound	455 g

GLOSSARY

baker's dozen: Thirteen of something. Originated among bakers and tradespeople who gave 13 items for a dozen, to prevent penalties from shorting people.

blind bake: A method to bake a pastry or pie shell by itself before adding a filling.

choux pastry: A pastry dough containing butter, water, flour, and eggs. Instead of a leavening agent (such as baking soda or baking powder), the dough rises because of the steam created from the high moisture content.

clafoutis: Sometimes spelled clafouti, it is a French dessert made with fruit such as cherries, and covered with a thick, flan-like batter.

confectioners' sugar: Finely powdered sugar, usually with cornstarch added. Also called powdered sugar.

crimp: A method of folding, pinching, and/or pleating the edges of a pie crust before baking. Similar to flute.

divided: When the same ingredient is used multiple times in different parts of a recipe.

dollop: A large spoonful of a soft food such as whipped cream.

en croûte: A French term for a food wrapped in some type of pastry dough and baked.

flute: The process of pressing a decorative pattern or design to the edges of a pie crust before baking.

fondant: a thick paste made of sugar, water, food coloring, and often flavoring oils or extracts used for icing and decorating cakes, cupcakes, and candies.

gluten: A mixture of proteins found in wheat and some grains. It makes dough elastic and helps the dough rise, keep its shape, and give a chewy texture to the baked dough.

gougères: A savory French baked good made out of choux pastry and cheese. Sometimes also stuffed with a savory filling.

kneading: Massaging or working the dough by stretching, folding, and pushing the dough to form gluten.

leaven: A substance (such as yeast, baking powder, and baking soda) that lightens dough or batter and causes it to rise.

mise en place: A French term that means "set in place" and is used in cooking to describe getting everything ready, such as ingredients and prep work, before you start cooking.

pâte à choux: See choux pastry.

pith: The white, bitter layer under the skin of some fruit, including citrus.

profiteroles: Small cream puffs that usually have a sweet or savory filling.

score: To cut lines into the surface of foods for a variety of reasons such as to help foods absorb more flavor or cook faster.

serrated: Notched or toothed on the end.

set: To become solid or firm.

tarte Tatin: A French apple tart that is generally baked with pastry on the top then turned over before serving.

tuiles: Thin, crisp French cookies that generally have a curved or rolled shape. They are formed while the cookies are still warm and allowed to cool to set.

zest: the outer colored part of citrus fruit peels. This part of the fruit contains oils that provide concentrated flavor.

RESOURCES

Listed below are some of my favorite sources for bakeware, serving dishes, specialty ingredients, kitchen gadgets, and more!

- Amazon
  www.amazon.com

- The Baker's Cupboard
  thebakerscupboard.com

- Bed, Bath & Beyond
  www.bedbathandbeyond.com

- Bob's Red Mill:
  www.bobsredmill.com

- Crate and Barrel
  www.crateandbarrel.com

- King Arthur Flour
  www.kingarthurflour.com

- Kitchen Collection
  www.kitchencollection.com

- Michael's
  www.michaels.com

- Penzeys
  www.penzeys.com

- Pampered Chef
  www.pamperedchef.com

- Pottery Barn
  www.potterybarn.com

- The Spice & Tea Exchange
  www.spiceandtea.com

- The Spice House
  www.thespicehouse.com

- Sur La Table
  www.surlatable.com

- West Elm
  www.westelm.com

- Williams-Sonoma
  www.williams-sonoma.com

- Wilton
  www.wilton.com

For more recipes, visit Snappy Gourmet at www.snappygourmet.com.

RECIPE INDEX

INDEX

ACKNOWLEDGMENTS

To my daughter, thank you for helping me in the kitchen every day testing recipes, always with a smile on your face. Your enthusiasm kept me going, and I enjoyed every minute baking with you!

To my son, thank you for always being my best taste tester. Your honest opinion and willingness to try anything and everything was extremely helpful.

To my husband, thank you for all your help cleaning up the big messes in the kitchen on a regular basis, even multiple times in one day.

To my mom and dad, thank you for always letting me cook, bake, and experiment in the kitchen when I was a kid.

To all my friends and neighbors, thank you for rushing over numerous times to be my taste testers.

To Meg, Elizabeth, Marthine, and the whole Callisto Media team, thank you for this fabulous opportunity and for all your help! I couldn't have done it without you all!

To Patty, thank you for knowing exactly what I was always trying to say, and thank you and your kids for testing the recipes and all your feedback!

CPSIA information can be obtained
at www.ICGtesting.com
Printed in the USA
BVOW11s0311021017

496137BV00001B/1/P

9 781623 159429